OLIVER GOLDSMITH

She Stoops to Conquer

Illustrated by

T. M. CLELAND

OLIVER GOLDSMITH

From a portrait by Sir Joshua Reynolds

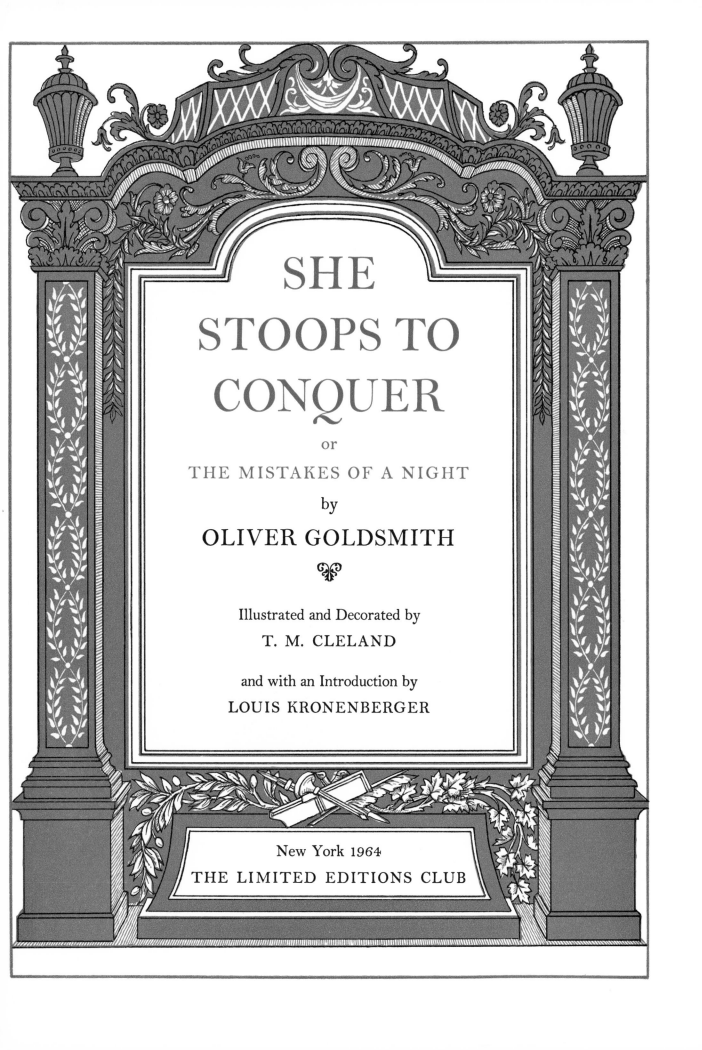

SHE
STOOPS TO
CONQUER

or

THE MISTAKES OF A NIGHT

by

OLIVER GOLDSMITH

Illustrated and Decorated by

T. M. CLELAND

and with an Introduction by

LOUIS KRONENBERGER

New York 1964
THE LIMITED EDITIONS CLUB

❊ INTRODUCTION ❊

OLIVER GOLDSMITH stands quite high in English literature, and a little apart, by reason of his three-pronged claims to recognition. There is his extremely famous poem, *The Deserted Village*; his extremely famous novel, *The Vicar of Wakefield*; his extremely famous play, *She Stoops to Conquer*. To have achieved three unquestioned classics that jointly run to about the length of an average-sized book is a notable example of how to travel down the ages with the lightest of luggage.

But though all three remain unquestioned classics, they no longer—if we are to be honest—enjoy a quite equal esteem or popularity. *The Deserted Village* has come to be a bit of a deserted poem. Certain of its lines and couplets have passed into the language, their authorship rather obscured; but the poem itself seems to be gradually passing out of circulation. Even as a high-school standby I suspect it is being replaced by something less pastoral and more vibrant. *The Vicar of Wakefield* has fared better, as it deserves to have done. For it has much of Goldsmith's kindliness and charm; and in any at all exhaustive journey through the English novel, one that stops at picturesque towns as well as populous cities, it must always have a place; it must, indeed—like *Cranford*, like *Our Village*—survive as the kind of

V

minor work whose value rests on its being minor. Its voice may not carry far, or instantly rivet attention, but it is a genuinely individual one.

But of Goldsmith's three classics, it seems pretty certain that *She Stoops to Conquer* is much the best entrenched. It has so unequivocally survived as to seem, again and again, worth reviving; only a short time ago the Phoenix Theatre revived it in New York. So long as actors eye juicy character parts, they must glance at Tony Lumpkin; so long as producers eye time-tried comic plots, they must give thought to Goldsmith's; and in *any* journey through the English comic theatre, even one confined to Principal Points of Interest, it must surely have a place. Between 1728 and the 1870's, which is to say between *The Beggar's Opera* and Gilbert and Sullivan, *The School for Scandal* and *The Rivals* are *its* only rivals; and *The Rivals*, to my mind, is its inferior. *She Stoops to Conquer* is an extraordinary work on a very odd basis: that, without there being anything the least bit extraordinary about it, it stands alone of its kind among the comic classics of the English stage. Surely there should be at least a dozen *She Stoops to Conquers*, a dozen farce comedies written between the age of Anne and the age of Victoria that, without ever seeming brilliant, are almost consistently lively; that, without ever turning bawdy, are not simpering or prim; that, with no great claim to wit, have a robust sense of fun; that, without being satirical, can spoof certain human weaknesses; and that, without being sentimental, remain friendly and good-natured.

Yet, unless they are moldering in unopened books on dust-covered shelves, far from there being a dozen such plays, where unmistakably is there another? What others manage (which is the crucial point) to sustain their good qualities throughout an entire evening? What others don't creep through a first act or crumble during the last, or don't plague us with a deadly sub-plot, or weary us with dialect jokes, or pelt us with petrified epigrams, or try our patience with spoonfuls of morality? *The Rivals*, for example, besides belonging to a different category or —what with mixing the satirical, the farcical, and the romantic —belonging to no category at all, makes us put up with Faulkland and Julia, who are decidedly bores. Goldsmith's lovers keep us far from breathless, but, by virtue of the uses Goldsmith puts them to, they are seldom boring.

Hence, instead of being recurrent in the English classic theatre, *She Stoops to Conquer* verges on the anomalous—a full evening's worth of good clean fun. It chiefly owes its vivacity, of course, to the farce idea that galvanizes it, the idea of having two young men directed to a private house—the very house they have been invited to visit—under the impression that it is an inn. The original title and surviving subtitle of the play, "The Mistakes of a Night," suggests the quick, cumulative nature of the plotting, and the frank nature of the farcicality. Goldsmith sticks to the possibilities in his hoax, which means that he ingeniously keeps exploring and extracting them.

Of just such a hoax had he himself, when very young, been a victim. He, too, seeking an inn, was directed by a practical joker to a private house; he, too, called for servants, and ordered supper, and left directions for breakfast. But with him the "landlord," knowing all the time who he was, kept a straight face and played a landlord's part, not enlightening the boy till he was leaving next morning. The experience could not but stick in his memory, could not—in so genuine a humorist—but grow and spread in his mind. Happily, unlike so many bits of amusing autobiography, this one had far more than anecdotal value; it had real stage value, it could flare with plot and flower into scenes.

It had particular stage value by virtue of its comic reversal of values. To mistake a private house for an inn, as against mistaking one private house for another, starts off with confusion on one side that can quickly spread to the other, and that creates not just personal misunderstandings but social "situations" and *gaffes*. And more during the eighteenth century than today, things that one was expected, was indeed encouraged, to do at an inn were the very things that were out of the question in a private house. At an inn a young gentleman might, indeed, not just give orders and make demands, but put the chatty landlord in his place and avoid his company and conversation. Moreover, it would be a kindness to encourage one's servants to drink as a way of running up a good-sized bill; and, given the situation, it would be automatic to mistake the daughter of the house for a barmaid. The plot thickens, of course, and the fun fattens by having the "landlord" stand aghast at the behavior of his guests; and the practical joke is kept going by the lubricating propinquity of the practical joker. Tony Lumpkin always stands ready to deceive or abet deception; no farce ever had more of a misleading man, whether at one moment by pretending to be in love with Miss Neville, or at another by driving Miss Neville and his mother over hill and dale in virtually their own backyard.

Tony, in the end, is much less a great character creation than a fat character part with pothouse tastes and prankster ways. But what is so lumpish in Tony is the more misleading thing about him: it conceals, it half denies, what is so sharp-witted. His mind must not be inferred from his manners. He is a booby who lays booby traps for others; he is the card-table simpleton who walks off with the winnings. The scene where he pretends to think his mother is shamming about the stolen jewels reveals how little of a fool he is and how greatly (in the theatre, above all) he can contribute to the fun.

Goldsmith does very well by Tony, and by us, in giving him Mrs. Hardcastle for a doting mother; theirs is perhaps the most enjoyable relationship in the play. The two pairs of lovers are to be praised, I think, not so much for qualities of character as for so lightly and briskly advancing the plot. Even Marlow's being altogether at his ease with wenches and hopelessly shy with young ladies scores best as an amusing plot device. Plot, as it must be in farce, is the real motive power of the play. But it proves the saving grace of the play as well, in that the plot, really, always calls the tune, always sets the level, refusing to halt for any detailed picture of manners or for more than a surface coat of romance.

Nothing is better known than that in *She Stoops to Conquer*— as earlier in *The Good-Natur'd Man*—Goldsmith was waging an assault on the sentimental comedy that had held the boards for upwards of fifty years. And the comedy of *She Stoops to Conquer* quite escapes being sentimental. But this, it seems to me, is chiefly through favoring plot situations over personal ones; which means, in the end, through scamping flesh and blood no less than sighs and tears. And if *She Stoops to Conquer* also escapes seeming genteel, it is chiefly from a certain air of the bucolic and rowdy—a sort of taproom indecorum that conceals the total absence of boudoir indecency. Where, at the beginning of the eighteenth century, George Farquhar had let the hero of *The Constant Couple* mistake a private house for a bordello, Goldsmith scarcely suggests that *his* private house has bedrooms. But Farquhar's racier amusement lasts for only a scene or two (which is all the situation proves worth) and his play, as a whole, is decidedly mixed and uneven; whereas Goldsmith's situation does last out a whole play; and his effect, if on occasion tame, is never jumbled.

What in the long run has so much helped *She Stoops to Conquer* must at the outset have seemed destined to harm it—its old-fashioned countryfied look, its genial humorist's good nature, its lack of something very new that must come to seem dated, of something very chic that in time must seem tacky. *She Stoops to Conquer* has its incidental merits: its best dialogue is thoroughly bright, it makes observations not just sound but astute, it contains social details that are revealing and vivid. But such things are just frequent enough to remind us that Goldsmith was a real writer, a man of real parts and cultivation. At the same time they are unobtrusive enough not to halt the flow of the fun —that immemorial fun born of human beings at cross-purposes and of situations gone askew and awry. Never too resplendent when young, *She Stoops to Conquer* does not now look shiny with age. It has a picturesque rust, a coach-lamp rusticity; it offers, on stageworthy terms, that reverse side of the eighteenth century's gloss and high style—its jackbooted antics, its tankard-in-hand joviality.

LOUIS KRONENBERGER

xi

SHE STOOPS TO CONQUER

or

The Mistakes of a Night

DRAMATIS PERSONÆ

MEN

Sir Charles Marlow
Young Marlow (*his Son*)
Hardcastle
Hastings
Tony Lumpkin
Diggory

WOMEN

Mrs. Hardcastle
Miss Hardcastle
Miss Neville
Maid

Landlords, Servants, &c., &c.

ACT ONE

SCENE I—*A Chamber in an old-fashioned House*

Enter Mrs. Hardcastle *and* Mr. Hardcastle.

Mrs. Hardcastle. I vow, Mr. Hardcastle, you're very particular. Is there a creature in the whole country but ourselves that does not take a trip to town now and then, to rub off the rust a little? There's the two Miss Hoggs, and our neighbour, Mrs. Grigsby, go to take a month's polishing every winter.

Hardcastle. Ay, and bring back vanity and affectation to last them the whole year. I wonder why London cannot keep its own fools at home. In my time, the follies of the town crept slowly among us, but now they travel faster than a stage-coach. Its fopperies come down, not only as inside passengers, but in the very basket.

Mrs. Hardcastle. Ay, *your* times were fine times, indeed; you have been telling us of *them* for many a long year. Here we live in an old rambling mansion, that looks for all the world like an inn, but that we never see company. Our best visitors are old Mrs. Oddfish, the curate's wife, and little Cripplegate, the lame dancing-master: and all our entertainment your old stories of Prince Eugene and the Duke of Marlborough. I hate such old-fashioned trumpery.

Hardcastle. And I love it. I love every thing that's old: old friends, old times, old manners, old books, old wine; and, I believe, Dorothy [*taking her hand*], you'll own I have been pretty fond of an old wife.

Mrs. Hardcastle. Lord, Mr. Hardcastle, you're for ever at your Dorothy's and your old wife's. You may be a Darby, but I'll be no Joan, I promise you. I'm not so old as you'd make me by more than one good year. Add twenty to twenty, and make money of that.

Hardcastle. Let me see; twenty added to twenty—makes just fifty and seven!

Mrs. Hardcastle. It's false, Mr. Hardcastle: I was but twenty when I was brought to bed of Tony, that I had by Mr. Lumpkin, my first husband; and he's not come to years of discretion yet.

Hardcastle. Nor ever will, I dare answer for him. Ay, you have taught *him* finely!

Mrs. Hardcastle. No matter, Tony Lumpkin has a good fortune. My son is not to live by his learning. I don't think a boy wants much learning to spend fifteen hundred a year.

Hardcastle. Learning, quotha! A mere composition of tricks and mischief!

Mrs. Hardcastle. Humour, my dear: nothing but humour. Come, Mr. Hardcastle, you must allow the boy a little humour.

Hardcastle. I'd sooner allow him a horse-pond! If burning the footmen's shoes, frightening the maids, and worrying the kittens, be humour, he has it. It was but yesterday he fastened my wig to the back of my chair, and when I went to make a bow, I popt my bald head in Mrs. Frizzle's face!

Mrs. Hardcastle. And am I to blame? The poor boy was always too sickly to do any good. A school would be his death. When he comes to be a little stronger, who knows what a year or two's Latin may do for him?

Hardcastle. Latin for him! A cat and fiddle! No, no, the ale-house and the stable are the only schools he'll ever go to.

Mrs. Hardcastle. Well, we must not snub the poor boy now, for I believe we shan't have him long among us. Any body that looks in his face may see he's consumptive.

Hardcastle. Ay, if growing too fat be one of the symptoms.

Mrs. Hardcastle. He coughs sometimes.

Hardcastle. Yes, when his liquor goes the wrong way.

Mrs. Hardcastle. I'm actually afraid of his lungs.

Hardcastle. And truly, so am I; for he sometimes whoops like a speaking trumpet—[Tony *hallooing behind the scenes.*]— O, there he goes—A very consumptive figure, truly!

Enter Tony, *crossing the stage.*

5

Mrs. Hardcastle. Tony, where are you going, my charmer? Won't you give papa and I a little of your company, lovee?

Tony. I'm in haste, mother, I cannot stay.

Mrs. Hardcastle. You shan't venture out this raw evening, my dear: you look most shockingly.

Tony. I can't stay, I tell you. *The Three Pigeons* expects me down every moment. There's some fun going forward.

Hardcastle. Ay; the ale-house, the old place: I thought so.

Mrs. Hardcastle. A low, paltry set of fellows.

Tony. Not so low, neither. There's Dick Muggins, the exciseman; Jack Slang, the horse doctor; Little Aminadab, that grinds the music box; and Tom Twist, that spins the pewter platter.

Mrs. Hardcastle. Pray, my dear, disappoint them for one night, at least.

Tony. As for disappointing *them*, I should not so much mind; but I can't abide to disappoint *myself*.

Mrs. Hardcastle [*Detaining him*]. You shan't go.

Tony. I will, I tell you.

Mrs. Hardcastle. I say you shan't.

Tony. We'll see which is strongest, your or I.

[*Exit, hauling her out.*

HARDCASTLE, *solus.*

Hardcastle. Ay, there goes a pair that only spoil each other. But is not the whole age in a combination to drive sense and discretion out of doors? There's my pretty darling, Kate; the fashions of the times have almost infected her too. By living a year or two in town, she is as fond of gauze and French frippery as the best of them.

Enter MISS HARDCASTLE.

Hardcastle. Blessings on my pretty innocence! Drest out as usual, my Kate! Goodness! What a quantity of superfluous silk hast thou got about thee, girl! I could never teach the fools of this age that the indigent world could be clothed out of the trimmings of the vain.

Miss Hardcastle. You know our agreement, sir. You allow

me the morning to receive and pay visits, and to dress in my own manner; and in the evening, I put on my housewife's dress, to please you.

Hardcastle. Well, remember, I insist on the terms of our agreement; and, by-the-bye, I believe I shall have occasion to try your obedience this very evening.

Miss Hardcastle. I protest, sir, I don't comprehend your meaning.

Hardcastle. Then, to be plain with you, Kate, I expect the young gentleman I have chosen to be your husband from town this very day. I have his father's letter, in which he informs me his son is set out, and that he intends to follow himself shortly after.

Miss Hardcastle. Indeed! I wish I had known something of this before. Bless me, how shall I behave? It's a thousand to one I shan't like him; our meeting will be so formal, and so like a thing of business that I shall find no room for friendship or esteem.

Hardcastle. Depend upon it, child, I'll never control your choice; but Mr. Marlow, whom I have pitched upon, is the son of my old friend, Sir Charles Marlow, of whom you have heard me talk so often. The young gentleman has been bred a scholar, and is designed for an employment in the service of his country. I am told he's a man of an excellent understanding.

Miss Hardcastle. Is he?

Hardcastle. Very generous.

Miss Hardcastle. I believe I shall like him.

Hardcastle. Young and brave.

Miss Hardcastle. I'm sure I shall like him.

Hardcastle. And very handsome.

Miss Hardcastle. My dear papa, say no more [*Kissing his hand*], he's mine, I'll have him!

Hardcastle. And, to crown all, Kate, he's one of the most bashful and reserved young fellows in all the world.

Miss Hardcastle. Eh! you have frozen me to death again. That word *reserved* has undone all the rest of his accomplishments. A reserved lover, it is said, always makes a suspicious husband.

Hardcastle. On the contrary, modesty seldom resides in a breast that is not enriched with nobler virtues. It was the very feature in his character that first struck me.

Miss Hardcastle. He must have more striking features to catch me, I promise you. However, if he be so young, so handsome, and so everything, as you mention, I believe he'll do still. I think I'll have him.

Hardcastle. Ay, Kate, but there is still an obstacle. It's more than an even wager, he may not have *you*.

Miss Hardcastle. My dear papa, why will you mortify one

so?—Well, if he refuses, instead of breaking my heart at his in-difference, I'll only break my glass for its flattery. Set my cap to some newer fashion, and look out for some less difficult admirer.

Hardcastle. Bravely resolved! In the mean time, I'll go pre-pare the servants for his reception; as we seldom see company, they want as much training as a company of recruits the first day's muster. [*Exit.*

Miss Hardcastle, *sola.*

Miss Hardcastle. Lud, this news of papa's puts me all in a flutter. *Young, handsome;* these he put last; but I put them fore-most. *Sensible, good-natured;* I like all that. But then *reserved,* and *sheepish,* that's much against him. Yet, can't he be cured of his timidity by being taught to be proud of his wife? Yes, and can't I—But I vow I'm disposing of the husband before I have secured the lover!

Enter Miss Neville.

Miss Hardcastle. I'm glad you're come, Neville, my dear. Tell me, Constance, how do I look this evening? Is there any thing whimsical about me? Is it one of my well-looking days, child? Am I in face today?

Miss Neville. Perfectly, my dear. Yet, now I look again—bless me!—surely no accident has happened among the canary birds or the gold-fishes? Has your brother or the cat been meddling? Or has the last novel been too moving?

10

Miss Hardcastle. No; nothing of all this. I have been threatened—I can scarce get it out—I have been threatened with a lover!

Miss Neville. And his name—

Miss Hardcastle. Is Marlow.

Miss Neville. Indeed!

Miss Hardcastle. The son of Sir Charles Marlow.

Miss Neville. As I live, the most intimate friend of Mr. Hastings, *my* admirer. They are never asunder. I believe you must have seen him when we lived in town.

Miss Hardcastle. Never.

Miss Neville. He's a very singular character, I assure you. Among women of reputation and virtue, he is the modestest man alive; but his acquaintance give him a very different character among creatures of another stamp: you understand me.

Miss Hardcastle. An odd character, indeed! I shall never be able to manage him. What shall I do? Pshaw, think no more of him, but trust to occurrences for success. But how goes on your own affair, my dear? Has my mother been courting you for my brother Tony, as usual?

Miss Neville. I have just come from one of our agreeable *tête-à-têtes.* She has been saying a hundred tender things, and setting off her pretty monster as the very pink of perfection.

Miss Hardcastle. And her partiality is such that she actually

11

thinks him so. A fortune like yours is no small temptation. Besides, as she has the sole management of it, I'm not surprised to see her unwilling to let it go out of the family.

Miss Neville. A fortune like mine, which chiefly consists in jewels, is no such mighty temptation. But at any rate, if my dear Hastings be but constant, I make no doubt to be too hard for her at last. However, I let her suppose that I am in love with her son, and she never once dreams that my affections are fixed upon another.

Miss Hardcastle. My good brother holds out stoutly. I could almost love him for hating you so.

Miss Neville. It is a good natured creature at bottom, and I'm sure would wish to see me married to any body but himself. But my aunt's bell rings for our afternoon's walk round the improvements. *Allons.* Courage is necessary, as our affairs are critical.

Miss Hardcastle. Would it were bed time and all were well.

[*Exeunt.*

Scene II—*An alehouse room. Several shabby fellows, with punch
and tobacco.* Tony *at the head of the table, a little higher than
the rest: a mallet in his hand.*

Omnes. Hurrea, hurrea, hurrea, bravo!

First Fellow. Now, gentlemen, silence for a song. The
'Squire is going to knock himself down for a song.

Omnes. Ay, a song, a song.

Tony. Then I'll sing you, gentlemen, a song I made upon this
ale-house, *The Three Pigeons.*

SONG
> *Let school-masters puzzle their brain,*
> > *With grammar, and nonsense, and learning;*
> *Good liquor, I stoutly maintain,*
> > *Gives* genus *a better discerning,*
> *Let them brag of their Heathenish Gods,*
> > *Their Lethes, their Styxes, and Stygians;*
> *Their Quis, and their Quæs, and their Quods,*
> > *They're all but a parcel of Pigeons.*
> > > *Toroddle, toroddle, toroll!*

> *When Methodist preachers come down,*
> > *A preaching that drinking is sinful,*

13

I'll wager the rascals a crown,
  They always preach best with a skinful.
But when you come down with your pence,
  For a slice of their scurvy religion,
I'll leave it to all men of sense,
  But you, my good friend, are the pigeon.
                Toroddle, toroddle, toroll!

Then come, put the jorum about,
  And let us be merry and clever,
Our hearts and our liquors are stout,
  Here's the Three Jolly Pigeons for ever.
Let some cry up woodcock or hare,
  Your bustards, your ducks, and your widgeons;
But of all the birds in the air,
  Here's a health to the Three Jolly Pigeons.
                Toroddle, toroddle, toroll!

Omnes. Bravo, bravo!

First Fellow. The 'Squire has got spunk in him.

Second Fellow. I loves to hear him sing, bekeays he never gives us nothing that's *low*.

Third Fellow. O damn any thing that's *low*, I cannot bear it!

Fourth Fellow. The genteel thing is the genteel thing at any

14

time. If so be that a gentleman bees in a concatenation accordingly.

Third Fellow. I like the maxum of it, Master Muggins. What, tho' I am obligated to dance a bear, a man may be a gentleman for all that. May this be my poison if my bear ever dances but to the very genteelest of tunes. *Water Parted*, or the minuet in *Ariadne*.

Second Fellow. What a pity it is the 'Squire is not come to his own. It would be well for all the publicans within ten miles round of him.

15

Tony. Ecod, and so it would, Master Slang. I'd then shew what it was to keep choice of company.

Second Fellow. O, he takes after his own father for that. To be sure, old 'Squire Lumpkin was the finest gentleman I ever set my eyes on. For winding the straight horn, or beating a thicket for a hare, or a wench, he never had his fellow. It was a saying in the place that he kept the best horses, dogs, and girls in the whole county.

Tony. Ecod, and when I'm of age, I'll be no bastard, I promise you. I have been thinking of Bett Bouncer and the miller's grey mare to begin with. But come, my boys, drink about and be merry, for you pay no reckoning. Well, Stingo, what's the matter?

Enter LANDLORD.

Landlord. There be two gentlemen in a post-chaise at the door. They have lost their way upo' the forest; and they are talking something about Mr. Hardcastle.

Tony. As sure as can be, one of them must be the gentleman that's coming down to court my sister. Do they seem to be Londoners?

Landlord. I believe they may. They look woundily like Frenchmen.

Tony. Then desire them to step this way, and I'll set them right in a twinkling. [*Exit* LANDLORD.] Gentlemen, as they mayn't be good enough company for you, step down for a moment, and I'll be with you in the squeezing of a lemon.

[Exeunt Mob.

T<small>ONY</small> *solus.*

Tony. Father-in-law has been calling me whelp and hound, this half year. Now, if I pleased, I could be so revenged upon the old grumbletonian. But then I'm afraid—afraid of what? I shall soon be worth fifteen hundred a year, and let him frighten me out of *that* if he can!

Enter L<small>ANDLORD</small>, *conducting* M<small>ARLOW</small> *and* H<small>ASTINGS</small>.

Marlow. What a tedious, uncomfortable day have we had of it! We were told it was but forty miles across the country, and we have come above threescore!

Hastings. And all, Marlow, from that unaccountable reserve of yours, that would not let us enquire more frequently on the way.

Marlow. I own, Hastings, I am unwilling to lay myself under an obligation to every one I meet; and often stand the chance of an unmannerly answer.

Hastings. At present, however, we are not likely to receive any answer.

Tony. No offence, gentlemen. But I'm told you have been

17

enquiring for one Mr. Hardcastle, in these parts. Do you know what part of the country you are in?

Hastings. Not in the least, sir, but should thank you for information.

Tony. Nor the way you came?

Hastings. No, sir; but if you can inform us—

Tony. Why, gentlemen, if you know neither the road you are going, nor where you are, nor the road you came, the first thing I have to inform you is, that—you have lost your way.

Marlow. We wanted no ghost to tell us that.

Tony. Pray, gentlemen, may I be so bold as to ask the place from whence you came?

Marlow. That's not necessary towards directing us where we are to go.

Tony. No offence; but question for question is all fair, you know. Pray, gentlemen, is not this same Hardcastle a cross-grain'd, old-fashion'd, whimsical fellow with an ugly face, a daughter, and a pretty son?

Hastings. We have not seen the gentleman, but he has the family you mention.

Tony. The daughter, a tall, trapesing, trolloping, talkative maypole— The son, a pretty, well-bred, agreeable youth, that every body is fond of!

Marlow. Our information differs in this. The daughter is said to be well-bred and beautiful; the son, an awkward booby, reared up and spoiled at his mother's apron-string.

Tony. He-he-hem—then, gentlemen, all I have to tell you is, that you won't reach Mr. Hardcastle's house this night, I believe.

Hastings. Unfortunate!

Tony. It's a damn'd long, dark, boggy, dirty, dangerous way. Stingo, tell the gentlemen the way to Mr. Hardcastle's;— [*winking upon the* LANDLORD] Mr. Hardcastle's of Quagmire Marsh, you understand me.

Landlord. Master Hardcastle's! Lack-a-daisy, my masters,

19

you're come a deadly deal wrong! When you came to the bottom of the hill, you should have cross'd down Squash-lane.

Marlow. Cross down Squash-lane!

Landlord. Then you were to keep straight forward 'till you came to four roads.

Marlow. Come to where four roads meet!

Tony. Ay, but you must be sure to take only one of them.

Marlow. O, sir, you're facetious.

Tony. Then, keeping to the right, you are to go sideways till you come upon Crack-skull Common: there you must look sharp for the track of the wheel, and go forward 'till you come to Farmer Murrain's barn. Coming to the farmer's barn, you are to turn to the right, and then to the left, and then to the right about again, till you find out the old mill—

Marlow. Zounds, man, we could as soon find out the longitude!

Hastings. What's to be done, Marlow?

Marlow. This house promises but a poor reception; though, perhaps, the landlord can accommodate us.

Landlord. Alack, master, we have but one spare bed in the whole house.

Tony. And to my knowledge, that's taken up by three lodgers already. [*After a pause in which the rest seem disconcerted.*] I have hit it. Don't you think, Stingo, our landlady could accommodate the gentlemen, by the fire-side, with—three chairs and a bolster?

Hastings. I hate sleeping by the fire-side.

Marlow. And I detest your three chairs and a bolster.

Tony. You do, do you?—then let me see—what—if you go on a mile further, to the Buck's Head; the old Buck's Head on the hill, one of the best inns in the whole county?

Hastings. O ho! so we have escaped an adventure for this night, however.

Landlord [*Apart to* Tony]. Sure, you ben't sending them to your father's as an inn, be you?

Tony. Mum, you fool, you. Let *them* find that out. [*To them.*] You have only to keep on straight forward till you come to a large old house by the roadside. You'll see a pair of large horns over the door. That's the sign. Drive up the yard, and call stoutly about you.

Hastings. Sir, we are obliged to you. The servants can't miss the way?

Tony. No, no; but I tell you, though, the landlord is rich, and going to leave off business; so he wants to be thought a gentleman, saving your presence, he! he! he! He'll be for giving you his company, and, ecod, if you mind him, he'll persuade you that his mother was an alderman, and his aunt a justice of peace!

Landlord. A troublesome old blade, to be sure; but a keeps as good wines and beds as any in the whole country.

Marlow. Well, if he supplies us with these, we shall want no further connexion. We are to turn to the right, did you say?

Tony. No, no; straight forward. I'll just step myself and shew you a piece of the way. [*To the* LANDLORD.] Mum.

Landlord. Ah, bless your heart, for a sweet, pleasant— damn'd mischievous son of a whore. 　　　　　　[*Exeunt.*

❦ ACT TWO ❧

SCENE—*An old-fashioned House*

Enter HARDCASTLE, *followed by three or four awkward* Servants.

HARDCASTLE. Well, I hope you're perfect in the table exercise I have been teaching you these three days. You all know your posts and your places, and can show that you have been used to good company without ever stirring from home.

Omnes. Ay, ay.

Hardcastle. When company comes, you are not to pop out and stare, and then run in again, like frightened rabbits in a warren.

Omnes. No, no.

Hardcastle. You, Diggory, whom I have taken from the barn, are to make a show at the side-table; and you, Roger, whom I have advanced from the plough, are to place yourself behind *my* chair. But you're not to stand so, with your hands in your pockets. Take your hands from your pockets, Roger; and from your head, you blockhead, you. See how Diggory carries his hands. They're a little too stiff, indeed, but that's no great matter.

Diggory. Ay, mind how I hold them. I learned to hold my hands this way, when I was upon drill for the militia. And so being upon drill—

Hardcastle. You must not be so talkative, Diggory. You must be all attention to the guests. You must hear us talk, and not think of talking; you must see us drink, and not think of drinking; you must see us eat, and not think of eating.

Diggory. By the laws, your worship, that's parfectly unpossible. Whenever Diggory sees yeating going forward, ecod, he's always wishing for a mouthful himself.

Hardcastle. Blockhead! Is not a belly-full in the kitchen as good as a belly-full in the parlour? Stay your stomach with that reflection.

Diggory. Ecod, I thank your worship, I'll make a shift to stay my stomach with a slice of cold beef in the pantry.

Hardcastle. Diggory, you are too talkative. Then, if I happen to say a good thing, or tell a good story at table, you must not all burst out a-laughing, as if you made part of the company.

Diggory. Then, ecod, your worship must not tell the story of Ould Grouse in the gun-room: I can't help laughing at that—he! he! he!—for the soul of me! We have laughed at that these twenty years—ha! ha! ha!

Hardcastle. Ha! ha! ha! The story is a good one. Well, honest Diggory, you may laugh at that—but still remember to be attentive. Suppose one of the company should call for a glass of wine, how will you behave? A glass of wine, sir, if you please [*to* DIGGORY]—Eh, why don't you move?

Diggory. Ecod, your worship, I never have courage till I see the eatables and drinkables brought upo' the table, and then I'm as bauld as a lion.

Hardcastle. What, will no body move?

First Servant. I'm not to leave this pleace.

Second Servant. I'm sure it's no pleace of mine.

Third Servant. Nor mine, for sartain.

Diggory. Wauns, and I'm sure it canna be mine.

Hardcastle. You numbskulls! and so, while, like your betters, you are quarrelling for places, the guests must be starved. O you dunces! I find I must begin all over again—but don't I hear a coach drive into the yard? To your posts, you blockheads! I'll go in the mean time and give my old friend's son a hearty reception at the gate. [*Exit* HARDCASTLE.

Diggory. By the elevens, my pleace is gone quite out of my head!

Roger. I know that my pleace is to be every where!

First Servant. Where the devil is mine?

Second Servant. My pleace is to be no where at all; and so Ize go about my business!

[*Exeunt* SERVANTS, *running about as if frightened, different ways.*

Enter SERVANT *with candles, showing in* MARLOW *and* HASTINGS.

Servant. Welcome, gentlemen, very welcome. This way.

Hastings. After the disappointments of the day, welcome once more, Charles, to the comforts of a clean room and a good fire. Upon my word, a very well-looking house; antique but creditable.

Marlow. The usual fate of a large mansion. Having first

ruined the master by good housekeeping, it at last comes to levy contributions as an inn.

Hastings. As you say, we passengers are to be taxed to pay all these fineries. I have often seen a good side-board, or a marble chimney-piece, tho' not actually put in the bill, enflame a reckoning confoundedly.

Marlow. Travelers, George, must pay in all places. The only difference is that in good inns you pay dearly for luxuries; in bad inns you are fleeced and starved.

Hastings. You have lived pretty much among them. In truth, I have been often surprised that you who have seen so much of the world, with your natural good sense, and your many opportunities, could never yet acquire a requisite share of assurance.

Marlow. The Englishman's malady. But tell me, George, where could I have learned that assurance you talk of? My life has been chiefly spent in a college, or an inn, in seclusion from that lovely part of the creation that chiefly teach men confidence. I don't know that I was ever familiarly acquainted with a single modest woman—except my mother—But among females of another class, you know—

Hastings. Ay, among them you are impudent enough of all conscience!

Marlow. They are of *us*, you know.

Hastings. But in the company of women of reputation I never saw such an idiot, such a trembler; you look for all the world as if you wanted an opportunity of stealing out of the room.

Marlow. Why, man, that's because I *do* want to steal out of the room. Faith, I have often formed a resolution to break the ice, and rattle away at any rate. But I don't know how, a single glance from a pair of fine eyes has totally overset my resolutions. An impudent fellow may counterfeit modesty, but I'll be hanged if a modest man can ever counterfeit impudence.

Hastings. If you could but say half the fine things to them that I have heard you lavish upon the barmaid of an inn, or even a college bed maker—

Marlow. Why, George, I can't say fine things to them. They freeze, they petrify me. They may talk of a comet, or a burning mountain, or some such bagatelle. But to me, a modest woman, drest out in all her finery, is the most tremendous object of the whole creation.

Hastings. Ha! ha! ha! At this rate, man, how can you ever expect to marry!

Marlow. Never, unless, as among kings and princes, my bride were to be courted by proxy. If, indeed, like an Eastern bridegroom, one were to be introduced to a wife he never saw before, it might be endured. But to go through all the terrors of a formal courtship, together with the episode of aunts, grandmothers and cousins, and at last to blurt out the broad, staring question of,

Madam, will you marry me? No, no, that's a strain much above me, I assure you!

Hastings. I pity you. But how do you intend behaving to the lady you are come down to visit at the request of your father?

Marlow. As I behave to all other ladies. Bow very low. Answer yes, or no, to all her demands—But for the rest, I don't think I shall venture to look in her face till I see my father's again.

Hastings. I'm surprised that one who is so warm a friend can be so cool a lover.

Marlow. To be explicit, my dear Hastings, my chief inducement down was to be instrumental in forwarding your happiness, not my own. Miss Neville loves you, the family don't know you, as my friend you are sure of a reception, and let honour do the rest.

Hastings. My dear Marlow! But I'll suppress the emotion. Were I a wretch, meanly seeking to carry off a fortune, you should be the last man in the world I would apply to for assistance. But Miss Neville's person is all I ask, and that is mine, both from her deceased father's consent and her own inclination.

Marlow. Happy man! You have talents and art to captivate any woman. I'm doom'd to adore the sex, and yet to converse with the only part of it I despise. This stammer in my address, and this awkward, prepossessing visage of mine, can never per-

29

mit me to soar above the reach of a milliner's 'prentice, or one of the duchesses of Drury-lane.* Pshaw, this fellow here to interrupt us!

Enter HARDCASTLE.

Hardcastle. Gentlemen, once more you are heartily welcome. Which is Mr. Marlow? Sir, you're heartily welcome. It's not my way, you see, to receive my friends with my back to the fire. I like to give them a hearty reception, in the old style, at my gate. I like to see their horses and trunks taken care of.

Marlow [*Aside*]. He has got our names from the servants already. [*To him.*] We approve your caution and hospitality, sir. [*To* HASTINGS.] I have been thinking, George, of changing our travelling dresses in the morning. I am grown confoundedly ashamed of mine.

Hardcastle. I beg, Mr. Marlow, you'll use no ceremony in this house.

Hastings. I fancy, George, you're right: the first blow is half the battle. I intend opening the campaign with the white and gold.

Hardcastle. Mr. Marlow—Mr. Hastings—gentlemen—pray be under no constraint in this house. This is Liberty-hall, gentlemen. You may do just as you please here.

Marlow. Yet, George, if we open the campaign too fiercely

at first, we may want ammunition before it is over. I think to reserve the embroidery to secure a retreat.

Hardcastle. Your talking of a retreat, Mr. Marlow, puts me in mind of the Duke of Marlborough, when we went to besiege Denain. He first summoned the garrison—

Marlow. Don't you think the *ventre d'or* waistcoat will do with the plain brown?

Hardcastle. He first summoned the garrison, which might consist of about five thousand men—

Hastings. I think not: brown and yellow mix but very poorly.

Hardcastle. I say, gentlemen, as I was telling you, he summoned the garrison, which might consist of about five thousand men—

Marlow. The girls like finery.

Hardcastle. Which might consist of about five thousand men, well appointed with stores, ammunition, and other implements of war. "Now," says the Duke of Marlborough to George Brooks, that stood next to him—you must have heard of George Brooks; "I'll pawn my dukedom," says he, "but I take that garrison without spilling a drop of blood!" So—

Marlow. What, my good friend, if you gave us a glass of punch in the mean time; it would help us to carry on the siege with vigour.

Hardcastle [*Aside*]. Punch, sir!—This is the most unaccountable kind of modesty I ever met with!

Marlow. Yes, sir, punch! A glass of warm punch, after our journey, will be comfortable. This is Liberty-hall, you know.

Hardcastle. Here's cup, sir.

Marlow [*Aside*]. So this fellow, in his Liberty-hall, will only let us have just what he pleases.

Hardcastle [*Taking the cup*]. I hope you'll find it to your mind. I have prepared it with my own hands, and I believe you'll own the ingredients are tolerable. Will you be so good as to pledge me, sir? Here, Mr. Marlow, here is to our better acquaintance! [*Drinks.*

Marlow [*Aside*]. A very impudent fellow this! But he's a character, and I'll humour him a little.—Sir, my service to you.
[*Drinks.*

Hastings [*Aside*]. I see this fellow wants to give us his company, and forgets that he's an innkeeper before he has learned to be a gentleman.

Marlow. From the excellence of your cup, my old friend, I suppose you have a good deal of business in this part of the country. Warm work, now and then, at elections, I suppose?

Hardcastle. No, sir, I have long given that work over. Since our betters have hit upon the expedient of electing each other, there's no business *for us that sell ale.*

Hastings. So, then you have no turn for politics, I find.

Hardcastle. Not in the least. There was a time, indeed, I fretted myself about the mistakes of government, like other people; but, finding myself every day grow more angry, and the government growing no better, I left it to mend itself. Since that, I no more trouble my head about *Heyder Ally*, or *Ally Cawn*, than about *Ally Croaker.** Sir, my service to you.

Hastings. So that, with eating above stairs, and drinking below, with receiving your friends within, and amusing them without, you lead a good, pleasant, bustling life of it.

*The first two were Indian rulers; the last was a popular Irish song.

33

Hardcastle. I do stir about a great deal, that's certain. Half the differences of the parish are adjusted in this very parlour.

Marlow [*After drinking*]. And you have an argument in your cup, old gentleman, better than any in Westminster-hall.

Hardcastle. Ay, young gentleman, that, and a little philosophy.

Marlow [*Aside*]. Well, this is the first time I ever heard of an innkeeper's philosophy.

Hastings. So then, like an experienced general, you attack them on every quarter. If you find their reason manageable, you attack it with your philosophy; if you find they have no reason, you attack them with this. Here's your health, my philosopher.

[*Drinks*.

Hardcastle. Good, very good, thank you; ha! ha! Your generalship puts me in mind of Prince Eugene, when he fought the Turks at the battle of Belgrade. You shall hear—

Marlow. Instead of the battle of Belgrade, I believe it's almost time to talk about supper. What has your philosophy got in the house for supper?

Hardcastle [*Aside*]. For supper, sir!—Was ever such a request to a man in his own house!

Marlow. Yes, sir, supper, sir; I begin to feel an appetite. I shall make devilish work to-night in the larder, I promise you.

Hardcastle [*Aside*]. Such a brazen dog, sure, never my eyes beheld. [*To him.*] Why, really, sir, as for supper I can't well tell. My Dorothy, and the cook maid, settle these things between them. I leave these kind of things entirely to them.

Marlow. You do, do you?

Hardcastle. Entirely. By-the-bye, I believe they are in actual consultation upon what's for supper this moment in the kitchen.

Marlow. Then I beg they'll admit *me* as one of their privy council. It's a way I have got. When I travel, I always choose to regulate my own supper. Let the cook be called. No offence, I hope, sir.

Hardcastle. O, no, sir, none in the least; yet, I don't know how: our Bridget, the cook maid, is not very communicative upon these occasions. Should we send for her, she might scold us all out of the house.

Hastings. Let's see your list of the larder, then. I ask it as a favour. I always match my appetite to my bill of fare.

Marlow. [*To* HARDCASTLE, *who looks at them with surprise*]. Sir, he's very right, and it's my way too.

Hardcastle. Sir, you have a right to command here. Here, Roger, bring us the bill of fare for to-night's supper. I believe it's drawn out. [*Exit* ROGER.] Your manner, Mr. Hastings, puts me in mind of my uncle, Colonel Wallop. It was a saying of his that no man was sure of his supper till he had eaten it.

Hastings [*Aside*]. All upon the high ropes! His uncle a

colonel! We shall soon hear of his mother being a justice of peace. [*Re-enter* ROGER.] But let's hear the bill of fare.

Marlow [*Perusing*]. What's here? For the first course; for the second course; for the dessert. The devil, sir, do you think we have brought down the whole Joiners Company, or the Corporation of Bedford, to eat up such a supper? Two or three little things, clean and comfortable, will do.

Hastings. But let's hear it.

Marlow [*Reading*]. For the first course, at the top, a pig, and prune sauce.

Hastings. Damn your pig, I say!

Marlow. And damn your prune sauce, say I!

Hardcastle. And yet, gentlemen, to men that are hungry pig with prune sauce is very good eating.

Marlow. At the bottom, a calve's tongue and brains.

Hastings. Let your brains be knock'd out, my good sir; I don't like them.

Marlow. Or you may clap them on a plate by themselves. I do.

Hardcastle [*Aside*]. Their impudence confounds me. [*To them.*] Gentlemen, you are my guests, make what alterations you please. Is there any thing else you wish to retrench or alter, gentlemen?

Marlow. Item: a pork pie, a boiled rabbit and sausages, a florentine, a shaking pudding, and a dish of tiff—taff—taffety cream!

Hastings. Confound your made dishes! I shall be as much at a loss in this house as at a green and yellow dinner at the French Ambassador's table. I'm for plain eating.

Hardcastle. I'm sorry, gentlemen, that I have nothing you like, but if there be any thing you have a particular fancy to—

Marlow. Why, really, sir, your bill of fare is so exquisite that any one part of it is full as good as another. Send us what you please. So much for supper. And now to see that our beds are air'd and properly taken care of.

Hardcastle. I entreat you'll leave all that to me. You shall not stir a step.

Marlow. Leave that to you! I protest, sir, you must excuse me, I always look to these things myself.

Hardcastle. I must insist, sir, you'll make yourself easy on that head.

Marlow [*Aside*]. You see I'm resolved on it.—A very troublesome fellow this, as ever I met with.

Hardcastle [*Aside*]. Well, sir, I'm resolved at least to attend you. This may be modern modesty, but I never saw any thing look so like old-fashioned impudence.

[*Exeunt* MARLOW *and* HARDCASTLE.

HASTINGS, *solus.*

Hastings. So I find this fellow's civilities begin to grow troublesome. But who can be angry at those assiduities which are meant to please him? Ha! what do I see? Miss Neville, by all that's happy!

Enter MISS NEVILLE.

Miss Neville. My dear Hastings! To what unexpected good fortune, to what accident, am I to ascribe this happy meeting?

Hastings. Rather let me ask the same question, as I could never have hoped to meet my dearest Constance at an inn.

Miss Neville. An inn! Sure you mistake! My aunt, my guardian, lives here. What could induce you to think this house an inn?

Hastings. My friend, Mr. Marlow, with whom I came down, and I, have been sent here as to an inn, I assure you. A young fellow whom we accidentally met at a house hard by directed us hither.

Miss Neville. Certainly it must be one of my hopeful cousin's tricks, of whom you have heard me talk so often, ha! ha! ha! ha!

Hastings. He whom your aunt intends for you? He of whom I have such just apprehensions?

Miss Neville. You have nothing to fear from him, I assure you. You'd adore him if you knew how heartily he despises me. My aunt knows it too, and has undertaken to court me for him, and actually begins to think she has made a conquest.

Hastings. Thou dear dissembler! You must know, my Constance, I have just seized this happy opportunity of my friend's visit here to get admittance into the family. The horses that carried us down are now fatigued with their journey, but they'll soon be refreshed; and then, if my dearest girl will trust in her faithful Hastings, we shall soon be landed in France, where even among slaves the laws of marriage are respected.

Miss Neville. I have often told you, that though ready to obey you, I yet should leave my little fortune behind with reluctance. The greatest part of it was left me by my uncle, the India Director, and chiefly consists in jewels. I have been for some time persuading my aunt to let me wear them. I fancy I'm very near succeeding. The instant they are put into my possession you shall find me ready to make them and myself yours.

Hastings. Perish the baubles! Your person is all I desire. In the meantime, my friend Marlow must not be let into his mistake. I know the strange reserve of his temper is such that, if abruptly informed of it, he would instantly quit the house before our plan was ripe for execution.

Miss Neville. But how shall we keep him in the deception? Miss Hardcastle is just returned from walking; what if we still continue to deceive him?—This, this way—   [*They confer.*

Enter MARLOW.

Marlow. The assiduities of these good people tease me beyond bearing. My host seems to think it ill manners to leave me alone, and so he claps not only himself but his old-fashioned wife on my back. They talk of coming to sup with us, too; and then, I suppose, we are to run the gauntlet thro' all the rest of the family—What have we got here!—

Hastings. My dear Charles! Let me congratulate you!—The most fortunate accident! Who do you think is just alighted?

Marlow. Cannot guess.

Hastings. Our mistresses, boy, Miss Hardcastle and Miss Neville. Give me leave to introduce Miss Constance Neville to your acquaintance. Happening to dine in the neighbourhood, they called, on their return, to take fresh horses, here. Miss Hardcastle has just stept into the next room, and will be back in an instant. Wasn't it lucky? eh!

Marlow [*Aside*]. I have just been mortified enough of all conscience, and here comes something to complete my embarrassment.

Hastings. Well! but wasn't it the most fortunate thing in the world?

Marlow. Oh, yes! Very fortunate—a most joyful encounter—But our dresses, George, you know, are in disorder—What if we should postpone the happiness 'till to-morrow?—To-morrow at her own house—It will be every bit as convenient—And rather more respectful—To-morrow let it be. [*Offering to go.*

Miss Neville. By no means, sir. Your ceremony will displease her. The disorder of your dress will show the ardour of your impatience. Besides, she knows you are in the house, and will permit you to see her.

Marlow. O, the devil! how shall I support it? Hem! hem! Hastings, you must not go. You are to assist me, you know. I shall be confoundedly ridiculous. Yet, hang it, I'll take courage! Hem!

41

Hastings. Pshaw, man, it's but the first plunge, and all's over! She's but a woman, you know.

Marlow. And of all women she that I dread most to encounter!

Enter Miss Hardcastle, *as returned from walking, a bonnet, & c.*

Hastings [*Introducing them*]. Miss Hardcastle, Mr. Marlow; I'm proud of bringing two persons of such merit together, that only want to know, to esteem each other.

Miss Hardcastle [*Aside*]. Now for meeting my modest gentleman with a demure face, and quite in his own manner.

[*After a pause, in which he appears very uneasy and disconcerted.*] I'm glad of your safe arrival, sir—I'm told you had some accidents by the way.

Marlow. Only a few, madam. Yes, we had some. Yes, madam, a good many accidents, but should be sorry—madam— or rather glad of any accidents—that are so agreeably concluded. Hem!

Hastings [*To him*]. You never spoke better in your whole life. Keep it up, and I'll insure you the victory.

Miss Hardcastle. I'm afraid you flatter, sir. You that have seen so much of the finest company can find little entertainment in an obscure corner of the country.

Marlow [*Gathering courage*]. I have lived, indeed, in the world, madam; but I have kept very little company. I have been but an observer upon life, madam, while others were enjoying it.

Miss Neville. But that, I am told, is the way to enjoy it at last.

Hastings [*To him*]. Cicero never spoke better. Once more, and you are confirm'd in assurance for ever.

Marlow [*To him*]. Hem! Stand by me, then, and when I'm down, throw in a word or two to set me up again.

Miss Hardcastle. An observer, like you, upon life, were, I fear, disagreeably employed, since you must have had much more to censure than to approve.

Marlow. Pardon me, madam. I was always willing to be amused. The folly of most people is rather an object of mirth than uneasiness.

Hastings [*To him*]. Bravo, bravo. Never spoke so well in your whole life. Well, Miss Hardcastle, I see that you and Mr. Marlow are going to be very good company. I believe our being here will but embarrass the interview.

Marlow. Not in the least, Mr. Hastings. We like your company of all things. [*To him.*] Zounds, George! sure you won't go? How can you leave us?

Hastings. Our presence will but spoil conversation, so we'll retire to the next room. [*To him.*] You don't consider, man, that we are to manage a little *tête-à-tête* of our own.

[*Exeunt* HASTINGS *with* MISS NEVILLE.

Miss Hardcastle [*After a pause*]. But you have not been wholly an observer, I presume, sir. The ladies, I should hope, have employed some part of your addresses.

Marlow [*Relapsing into timidity*]. Pardon me, madam, I—I—I—as yet have studied—only—to—deserve them.

Miss Hardcastle. And that, some say, is the very worst way to obtain them.

Marlow. Perhaps so, madam. But I love to converse only with the more grave and sensible part of the sex—But I'm afraid I grow tiresome.

44

Miss Hardcastle. Not at all, sir; there is nothing I like so much as grave conversation myself: I could hear it for ever. Indeed, I have often been surprised how a man of *sentiment* could ever admire those light, airy pleasures, where nothing reaches the heart.

Marlow. It's—a disease—of the mind, madam. In the variety of tastes there must be some who, wanting a relish for— um-a-um.

Miss Hardcastle. I understand you, sir. There must be some, who, wanting a relish for refined pleasures, pretend to despise what they are incapable of tasting.

Marlow. My meaning, madam, but infinitely better expressed. And I can't help observing—a—

Miss Hardcastle [*Aside*]. Who could ever suppose this fellow impudent upon some occasions. [*To him.*] You were going to observe, sir—

Marlow. I was observing, madam—I protest, madam, I forget what I was going to observe.

Miss Hardcastle [*Aside*]. I vow and so do I. [*To him.*] You were observing, sir, that in this age of hypocrisy—something about hypocrisy, sir.

Marlow. Yes, madam. In this age of hypocrisy, there are few who upon strict enquiry do not—a—a—a—

Miss Hardcastle. I understand you perfectly, sir.

Marlow [*Aside*]. Egad, and that's more than I do myself!

Miss Hardcastle. You mean that in this hypocritical age there are few that do not condemn in public what they practise in private, and think they pay every debt to virtue when they praise it.

Marlow. True, madam; those who have most virtue in their mouths have least of it in their bosoms. But I'm sure I tire you, madam.

Miss Hardcastle. Not in the least, sir; there's something so agreeable and spirited in your manner, such life and force—pray, sir, go on.

Marlow. Yes, madam. I was saying—that there are some occasions—when a total want of courage, madam, destroys all the—and puts us—upon a—a—a—

Miss Hardcastle. I agree with you entirely: a want of courage upon some occasions assumes the appearance of ignorance, and betrays us when we most want to excel. I beg you'll proceed.

Marlow. Yes, madam. Morally speaking, madam—but I see Miss Neville expecting us in the next room. I would not intrude for the world.

Miss Hardcastle. I protest, sir, I never was more agreeably entertained in all my life. Pray, go on.

Marlow. Yes, madam. I was—but she beckons us to join her. Madam, shall I do myself the honour to attend you?

Miss Hardcastle. Well, then, I'll follow.

Marlow [Aside]. This pretty smooth dialogue has done for me.   [*Exit.*

MISS HARDCASTLE, *sola.*

Miss Hardcastle. Ha! ha! ha! Was there ever such a sober, sentimental interview? I'm certain he scarce look'd in my face the whole time. Yet the fellow, but for his unaccountable bashfulness, is pretty well too. He has good sense, but then so buried in his fears that it fatigues one more than ignorance. If I could teach him a little confidence, it would be doing somebody that I know of a piece of service. But who is that somebody?—that, faith, is a question I can scarce answer.   [*Exit.*

Enter TONY *and* MISS NEVILLE, *followed by* MRS. HARDCASTLE *and* HASTINGS.

Tony. What do you follow me for, Cousin Con? I wonder you're not ashamed to be so very engaging.

Miss Neville. I hope, cousin, one may speak to one's own relations, and not be to blame.

Tony. Ay, but I know what sort of a relation you want to make me, though; but it won't do. I tell you, Cousin Con, it won't do; so I beg you'll keep your distance. I want no nearer relationship.   [*She follows, coquetting him, to the back scene.*

Mrs. Hardcastle. Well! I vow, Mr. Hastings, you are very

47

entertaining. There's nothing in the world I love to talk of so much as London, and the fashions, though I was never there myself.

Hastings. Never there! You amaze me! From your air and manner, I concluded you had been bred all your life either at Ranelagh, St. James's, or Tower Wharf.*

*High- and low-class places are mixed here and in the next speech.

Mrs. Hardcastle. O, sir! you're only pleased to say so. We country persons can have no manner at all. I'm in love with the town, and that serves to raise me above some of our neighbouring rustics; but who can have a manner that has never seen the Pantheon, the Grotto Gardens, the Borough, and such places where the nobility chiefly resort? All I can do is to enjoy London at second-hand. I take care to know every *tête-à-tête* from the *Scandalous Magazine*, and have all the fashions as they come out, in a letter from the two Miss Rickets of Crooked-lane. Pray how do you like this head, Mr. Hastings?

Hastings. Extremely elegant and *dégagée*, upon my word, madam. Your friseur is a Frenchman, I suppose?

Mrs. Hardcastle. I protest, I dressed it myself from a print in the *Ladies Memorandum-book* for the last year.

Hastings. Indeed. Such a head in a side-box, at the Playhouse, would draw as many gazers as my Lady May'ress at a City Ball.

Mrs. Hardcastle. I vow, since inoculation began, there is no such thing to be seen as a plain woman; so one must dress a little particular or one may escape in the crowd.

Hastings. But that can never be your case, madam, in any dress! [*Bowing.*]

Mrs. Hardcastle. Yet, what signifies *my* dressing when I have such a piece of antiquity by my side as Mr. Hardcastle: all I can say will never argue down a single button from his clothes. I have often wanted him to throw off his great flaxen wig, and where he was bald, to plaster it over, like my Lord Pately, with powder.

Hastings. You are right, madam: for, as among the ladies there are none ugly, so among the men there are none old.

Mrs. Hardcastle. But what do you think his answer was? Why, with his usual Gothic vivacity, he said I only wanted him to throw off his wig to convert it into a *tête* for my own wearing!

Hastings. Intolerable! At your age you may wear what you please, and it must become you.

Mrs. Hardcastle. Pray, Mr. Hastings, what do you take to be the most fashionable age about town?

Hastings. Some time ago forty was all the mode; but I'm told the ladies intend to bring up fifty for the ensuing winter.

Mrs. Hardcastle. Seriously? Then I shall be too young for the fashion!

Hastings. No lady begins now to put on jewels 'till she's past forty. For instance, miss there, in a polite circle, would be considered as a child, as a mere maker of samplers.

Mrs. Hardcastle. And yet Mrs. Niece thinks herself as much a woman, and is as fond of jewels as the oldest of us all.

Hastings. Your niece, is she? And that young gentleman,—a brother of yours, I should presume?

Mrs. Hardcastle. My son, sir. They are contracted to each other. Observe their little sports. They fall in and out ten times a day, as if they were man and wife already. [*To them.*] Well, Tony, child, what soft things are you saying to your Cousin Constance, this evening?

Tony. I have been saying no soft things; but that it's very hard to be followed about so. Ecod! I've not a place in the house now that's left to myself but the stable.

Mrs. Hardcastle. Never mind him, Con, my dear. He's in another story behind your back.

Miss Neville. There's something generous in my cousin's manner. He falls out before faces to be forgiven in private.

Tony. That's a damned confounded—crack.

Mrs. Hardcastle. Ah, he's a sly one! Don't you think they're like each other about the mouth, Mr. Hastings? The Blenkinsop mouth to a T. They're of a size too. Back to back, my pretties, that Mr. Hastings may see you. Come, Tony.

Tony. You had as good not make me, I tell you.

[*Measuring.*

50

Miss Neville. O lud! he has almost cracked my head.

Mrs. Hardcastle. O, the monster! For shame, Tony. You a man, and behave so!

Tony. If I'm a man, let me have my fortune. Ecod! I'll not be made a fool of no longer.

Mrs. Hardcastle. Is this, ungrateful boy, all that I'm to get for the pains I have taken in your education? I that have rock'd you in your cradle, and fed that pretty mouth with a spoon! Did not I work that waistcoat to make you genteel? Did not I prescribe for you every day, and weep while the receipt was operating?

Tony. Ecod! you had reason to weep, for you have been dosing me ever since I was born. I have gone through every receipt in the Complete Housewife ten times over; and you have thoughts of coursing me through *Quincy* next spring. But, ecod! I tell you, I'll not be made a fool of no longer.

Mrs. Hardcastle. Wasn't it all for your good, viper? Wasn't it all for your good?

Tony. I wish you'd let me and my good alone, then. Snubbing this way when I'm in spirits. If I'm to have any good, let it come of itself; not to keep dinging it, dinging it into one so.

Mrs. Hardcastle. That's false; I never see you when you're in spirits. No, Tony, you then go to the ale house or kennel. I'm never to be delighted with your agreeable wild notes, unfeeling monster.

Tony. Ecod, Mamma, your own notes are the wildest of the two!

Mrs. Hardcastle. Was ever the like? But I see he wants to break my heart, I see he does.

Hastings. Dear madam, permit me to lecture the young gentleman a little. I'm certain I can persuade him to his duty.

Mrs. Hardcastle. Well! I must retire. Come Constance, my love. You see, Mr. Hastings, the wretchedness of my situation. Was ever poor woman so plagued with a dear, sweet, pretty, provoking, undutiful boy.

[*Exeunt* Mrs. Hardcastle *and* Miss Neville.

Tony [*Singing*]. *There was a young man riding by, and fain would have his will. Rang do didlo dee.* Don't mind her. Let her

cry. It's the comfort of her heart. I have seen her and sister cry over a book for an hour together, and they said they liked the book the better the more it made them cry.

Hastings. Then you're no friend to the ladies, I find, my pretty young gentleman?

Tony. That's as I find 'um.

Hastings. Not to her of your mother's choosing, I dare answer? And yet she appears to me a pretty, well-tempered girl.

Tony. That's because you don't know her as well as I. Ecod! I know every inch about her; and there's not a more bitter, cantankerous toad in all Christendom!

Hastings. [*Aside*]. Pretty encouragement, this, for a lover!

Tony. I have seen her since the height of that. She has as many tricks as a hare in a thicket, or a colt the first day's breaking.

Hastings. To me she appears sensible and silent!

Tony. Ay, before company. But when she's with her playmates, she's as loud as a hog in a gate.

Hastings. But there is a meek modesty about her that charms me.

Tony. Yes, but curb her never so little, she kicks up, and you're flung in a ditch.

Hastings. Well, but you must allow her a little beauty. —Yes, you must allow her some beauty.

Tony. Bandbox! She's all a made up thing, mun. Ah! could you but see Bet Bouncer of these parts, you might then talk of beauty. Ecod, she has two eyes as black as sloes, and cheeks as broad and red as a pulpit cushion. She'd make two of she.

Hastings. Well, what say you to a friend that would take this bitter bargain off your hands?

Tony. Anon.

Hastings. Would you thank him that would take Miss Neville, and leave you to happiness and your dear Betsy?

Tony. Ay; but where is there such a friend, for who would take *her?*

Hastings. I am he. If you but assist me, I'll engage to whip her off to France, and you shall never hear more of her.

Tony. Assist you! Ecod, I will, to the last drop of my blood. I'll clap a pair of horses to your chaise that shall trundle you off in a twinkling, and may be get you a part of her fortune besides, in jewels, that you little dream of.

Hastings. My dear Squire, this looks like a lad of spirit.

Tony. Come along then, and you shall see more of my spirit before you have done with me.   [*Singing.*

    We are the boys
    That fears no noise
    Where the thundering cannons roar.   [*Exeunt.*

❦ ACT THREE ❦

Scene—*The House*

Enter Hardcastle, *solus*.

Hardcastle. What could my old friend Sir Charles mean by recommending his son as the modestest young man in town? To me he appears the most impudent piece of brass that ever spoke with a tongue. He has taken possession of the easy chair by the fire-side already. He took off his boots in the parlour, and desired me to see them taken care of. I'm desirous to know how his impudence affects my daughter.—She will certainly be shocked at it.

Enter Miss Hardcastle, *plainly dressed*.

Hardcastle. Well, my Kate, I see you have changed your dress as I bid you; and yet, I believe, there was no great occasion.

Miss Hardcastle. I find such a pleasure, sir, in obeying your commands, that I take care to observe them without ever debating their propriety.

Hardcastle. And yet, Kate, I sometimes give you some cause,

particularly when I recommended my *modest* gentleman to you as a lover to-day.

Miss Hardcastle. You taught me to expect something extraordinary, and I find the original exceeds the description!

Hardcastle. I was never so surprised in my life! He has quite confounded all my faculties!

Miss Hardcastle. I never saw any thing like it! And a man of the world, too!

Hardcastle. Ay, he learned it all abroad,—what a fool was I, to think a young man could learn modesty by travelling. He might as soon learn wit at a masquerade.

56

Miss Hardcastle. It seems all natural to him.

Hardcastle. A good deal assisted by bad company and a French dancing-master.

Miss Hardcastle. Sure, you mistake, papa! a French dancing-master could never have taught him that timid look,—that awkward address,—that bashful manner—

Hardcastle. Whose look, whose manner, child?

Miss Hardcastle. Mr. Marlow's: his *mauvaise honte*, his timidity struck me at the first sight.

Hardcastle. Then your first sight deceived you; for I think him one of the most brazen first sights that ever astonished my senses!

Miss Hardcastle. Sure, sir, you rally! I never saw any one so modest.

Hardcastle. And can you be serious! I never saw such a bouncing, swaggering puppy since I was born. Bully Dawson was but a fool to him.

Miss Hardcastle. Surprising! He met me with a respectful bow, a stammering voice, and a look fixed on the ground.

Hardcastle. He met me with a loud voice, a lordly air, and a familiarity that made my blood freeze again.

Miss Hardcastle. He treated me with diffidence and respect; censured the manners of the age; admired the prudence of girls that never laughed; tired me with apologies for being tiresome;

then left the room with a bow, and, "Madam, I would not for the world detain you."

Hardcastle. He spoke to me as if he knew me all his life before. Asked twenty questions, and never waited for an answer. Interrupted my best remarks with some silly pun, and when I was in my best story of the Duke of Marlborough and Prince Eugene, he asked if I had not a good hand at making punch. Yes, Kate, he ask'd your father if he was a maker of punch!

Miss Hardcastle. One of us must certainly be mistaken.

Hardcastle. If he be what he has shown himself, I'm determined he shall never have my consent.

Miss Hardcastle. And if he be the sullen thing I take him, he shall never have mine.

Hardcastle. In one thing then we are agreed—to reject him.

Miss Hardcastle. Yes. But upon conditions. For if you should find him less impudent, and I more presuming; if you find him more respectful, and I more importunate—I don't know—the fellow is well enough for a man—Certainly we don't meet many such at a horse race in the country.

Hardcastle. If we should find him so—But that's impossible. The first appearance has done my business. I'm seldom deceived in that.

Miss Hardcastle. And yet there may be many good qualities under that first appearance.

Hardcastle. Ay, when a girl finds a fellow's outside to her taste, she then sets about guessing the rest of his furniture. With her, a smooth face stands for good sense, and a genteel figure for every virtue.

Miss Hardcastle. I hope, sir, a conversation begun with a compliment to my good sense won't end with a sneer at my understanding?

Hardcastle. Pardon me, Kate. But if young Mr. Brazen can find the art of reconciling contradictions, he may please us both, perhaps.

Miss Hardcastle. And as one of us must be mistaken, what if we go to make further discoveries?

Hardcastle. Agreed. But depend on't I'm in the right.

Miss Hardcastle. And depend on't I'm not much in the wrong. [*Exeunt.*

Enter TONY, *running in with a casket.*

Tony. Ecod! I have got them. Here they are. My Cousin Con's necklaces, bobs and all. My mother shan't cheat the poor souls out of their fortune neither. O, my genus! is that you?

Enter HASTINGS.

Hastings. My dear friend, how have you managed with your mother? I hope you have amused her with pretending love for your cousin, and that you are willing to be reconciled at last?

Our horses will be refreshed in a short time, and we shall soon be ready to set off.

Tony. And here's something to bear your charges by the way,—[*Giving the casket*] your sweetheart's jewels. Keep them, and hang those, I say, that would rob you of one of them!

Hastings. But how have you procured them from your mother?

Tony. Ask me no questions, and I'll tell you no fibs. I procured them by the rule of thumb. If I had not a key to every drawer in mother's bureau, how could I go to the alehouse so often as I do? An honest man may rob himself of his own at any time.

Hastings. Thousands do it every day. But to be plain with you; Miss Neville is endeavouring to procure them from her aunt this very instant. If she succeeds, it will be the most delicate way at least of obtaining them.

Tony. Well, keep them, till you know how it will be. But I know how it will be well enough; she'd as soon part with the only sound tooth in her head!

Hastings. But I dread the effects of her resentment when she finds she has lost them.

Tony. Never you mind her resentment, leave *me* to manage that. I don't value her resentment the bounce of a cracker. Zounds! here they are! Morrice, Prance!   [*Exit* HASTINGS.

TONY, MRS. HARDCASTLE, MISS NEVILLE.

Mrs. Hardcastle. Indeed, Constance, you amaze me. Such a girl as you want jewels? It will be time enough for jewels, my dear, twenty years hence, when your beauty begins to want repairs.

Miss Neville. But what will repair beauty at forty will certainly improve it at twenty, madam.

Mrs. Hardcastle. Yours, my dear, can admit of none. That natural blush is beyond a thousand ornaments. Besides, child, jewels are quite out at present. Don't you see half the ladies of our acquaintance, my Lady Kill-daylight, and Mrs. Crump, and the rest of them, carry their jewels to town, and bring nothing but paste and marcasites back?

Miss Neville. But who knows, madam, but somebody that shall be nameless would like me best with all my little finery about me?

Mrs. Hardcastle. Consult your glass, my dear, and then see, if with such a pair of eyes, you want any better sparklers. What do you think, Tony, my dear, does your Cousin Con want any jewels, in your eyes, to set off her beauty?

Tony. That's as thereafter may be.

Miss Neville. My dear aunt, if you knew how it would oblige me.

Mrs. Hardcastle. A parcel of old-fashioned rose and table-cut things. They would make you look like the court of King Solomon at a puppet-show. Besides, I believe I can't readily come at them. They may be missing, for aught I know to the contrary.

Tony [*Apart to* Mrs. HARDCASTLE]. Then why don't you tell her so at once, as she's so longing for them. Tell her they're lost. It's the only way to quiet her. Say they're lost, and call me to bear witness.

Mrs. Hardcastle [*Apart to* TONY]. You know, my dear, I'm only keeping them for you. So if I say they're gone, you'll bear me witness, will you? He! he! he!

Tony [*Apart to* Mrs. HARDCASTLE]. Never fear me. Ecod! I'll say I saw them taken out with my own eyes.

Miss Neville. I desire them but for a day, madam. Just to be permitted to show them as relics, and then they may be lock'd up again.

Mrs. Hardcastle. To be plain with you, my dear Constance, if I could find them, you should have them. They're missing, I assure you. Lost, for aught I know; but we must have patience wherever they are.

Miss Neville. I'll not believe it; this is but a shallow pretence to deny me. I know they're too valuable to be so slightly kept, and as you are to answer for the loss.

Mrs. Hardcastle. Don't be alarm'd, Constance. If they be lost, I must restore an equivalent. But my son knows they are missing, and not to be found.

Tony. That I can bear witness to. They are missing, and not to be found, I'll take my oath on't.

Mrs. Hardcastle. You must learn resignation, my dear; for tho' we lose our fortune, yet we should not lose our patience. See me, how calm I am.

Miss Neville. Ay, people are generally calm at the misfortunes of others.

Mrs. Hardcastle. Now, I wonder a girl of your good sense should waste a thought upon such trumpery. We shall soon find them; and, in the mean time, you shall make use of my garnets till your jewels be found.

Miss Neville. I detest garnets!

Mrs. Hardcastle. The most becoming things in the world to set off a clear complexion. You have often seen how well they look upon me. You *shall* have them.   [*Exit.*

Miss Neville. I dislike them of all things. You shan't stir.—Was ever any thing so provoking,—to mislay my own jewels, and force me to wear her trumpery.

Tony. Don't be a fool. If she gives you the garnets, take what you can get. The jewels are your own already. I have stolen them out of her bureau, and she does not know it. Fly to your spark, he'll tell you more of the matter. Leave me to manage *her*.

Miss Neville. My dear cousin!

Tony. Vanish. She's here, and has missed them already. [*Exit* Miss Neville.] Zounds! how she fidgets and spits about like a Catherine wheel.

Enter Mrs. Hardcastle.

Mrs. Hardcastle. Confusion! thieves! robbers! We are cheated, plundered, broke open, undone!

Tony. What's the matter, what's the matter, mamma? I hope nothing has happened to any of the good family!

Mrs. Hardcastle. We are robbed. My bureau has been broke open, the jewels taken out, and I'm undone!

Tony. Oh! is that all? Ha! ha! ha! By the laws, I never saw it better acted in my life. Ecod, I thought you was ruin'd in earnest, ha, ha, ha!

Mrs. Hardcastle. Why, boy, I *am* ruined in earnest. My bureau has been broke open, and all taken away.

Tony. Stick to that; ha, ha, ha! stick to that. I'll bear witness, you know, call me to bear witness.

Mrs. Hardcastle. I tell you, Tony, by all that's precious, the jewels are gone, and I shall be ruin'd for ever.

Tony. Sure I know they're gone, and I am to say so.

65

Mrs. Hardcastle. My dearest Tony, but hear me. They're gone, I say.

Tony. By the laws, mamma, you make me for to laugh, ha! ha! I know who took them well enough, ha! ha! ha!

Mrs. Hardcastle. Was there ever such a blockhead, that can't tell the difference between jest and earnest. I tell you I'm not in jest, booby!

Tony. That's right, that's right! You must be in a bitter passion, and then nobody will suspect either of us. I'll bear witness that they are gone.

Mrs. Hardcastle. Was there ever such a cross-grain'd brute, that won't hear me! Can you bear witness that you're no better than a fool? Was ever poor woman so beset with fools on one hand, and thieves on the other?

Tony. I can bear witness to that.

Mrs. Hardcastle. Bear witness again, you blockhead, you, and I'll turn you out of the room directly. My poor niece, what will become of *her!* Do you laugh, you unfeeling brute, as if you enjoy'd my distress?

Tony. I can bear witness to that.

Mrs. Hardcastle. Do you insult me, monster? I'll teach you to vex your mother, I will!

Tony. I can bear witness to that.

[*He runs off; she follows him.*

66

ACT THREE

Enter MISS HARDCASTLE *and* MAID.

Miss Hardcastle. What an unaccountable creature is that brother of mine, to send them to the house as an inn, ha! ha! I don't wonder at his impudence.

Maid. But what is more, madam, the young gentleman as you passed by in your present dress, ask'd me if you were the bar maid? He mistook you for the bar maid, madam!

Miss Hardcastle. Did he? Then as I live I'm resolved to keep up the delusion. Tell me, Pimple, how do you like my present dress? Don't you think I look something like Cherry in the *Beaux' Stratagem?*

Maid. It's the dress, madam, that every lady wears in the country, but when she visits or receives company.

Miss Hardcastle. And are you sure he does not remember my face or person?

Maid. Certain of it!

Miss Hardcastle. I vow, I thought so; for though we spoke for some time together, yet his fears were such that he never once looked up during the interview. Indeed, if he had, my bonnet would have kept him from seeing me.

Maid. But what do you hope from keeping him in his mistake?

Miss Hardcastle. In the first place, I shall be *seen*, and that is no small advantage to a girl who brings her face to market. Then

I shall perhaps make an acquaintance, and that's no small victory gained over one who never addresses any but the wildest of her sex. But my chief aim is to take my gentleman off his guard, and like an invisible champion of romance examine the giant's force before I offer to combat.

Maid. But are you sure you can act your part, and disguise your voice, so that he may mistake that, as he has already mistaken your person?

Miss Hardcastle. Never fear me. I think I have got the true bar cant.—Did your honour call?—Attend the Lion there.—Pipes and tobacco for the Angel.—The Lamb has been outrageous this half hour!

Maid. It will do, madam. But he's here.   [*Exit* MAID.

Enter MARLOW.

Marlow. What a bawling in every part of the house; I have scarce a moment's repose. If I go to the best room, there I find my host and his story. If I fly to the gallery, there we have my hostess with her curtsey down to the ground. I have at last got a moment to myself, and now for recollection. [*Walks and muses.*

Miss Hardcastle. Did you call, sir? Did your honour call?

Marlow [*Musing*]. As for Miss Hardcastle, she's too grave and sentimental for me.

Miss Hardcastle. Did your honour call?

[She still places herself before him, he turning away.

Marlow. No, child! *[Musing.]* Besides, from the glimpse I had of her, I think she squints.

Miss Hardcastle. I'm sure, sir, I heard the bell ring.

Marlow. No, no! *[Musing.]* I have pleased my father, however, by coming down, and I'll to-morrow please myself by returning. *[Taking out his tablets, and perusing.*

Miss Hardcastle. Perhaps the other gentleman called, sir?

Marlow. I tell you no.

Miss Hardcastle. I should be glad to know, sir. We have such a parcel of servants.

Marlow. No, no, I tell you. *[Looks full in her face.]* Yes, child, I think I did call. I wanted—I wanted—I vow, child, you are vastly handsome!

Miss Hardcastle. O la, sir, you'll make one asham'd.

Marlow. Never saw a more sprightly, malicious eye. Yes, yes, my dear, I did call. Have you got any of your—a—what d'ye call it in the house?

Miss Hardcastle. No, sir, we have been out of that these ten days.

Marlow. One may call in this house, I find, to very little purpose. Suppose I should call for a taste, just by way of trial, of the nectar of your lips; perhaps I might be disappointed in that, too?

Miss Hardcastle. Nectar? nectar? that's a liquor there's no call for in these parts. French, I suppose. We keep no French wines here, sir.

Marlow. Of true English growth, I assure you.

Miss Hardcastle. Then it's odd I should not know it. We brew all sorts of wines in this house, and I have lived here these eighteen years.

Marlow. Eighteen years! Why one would think, child, you kept the bar before you were born. How old are you?

Miss Hardcastle. O! sir, I must not tell my age. They say women and music should never be dated.

Marlow. To guess at this distance, you can't be much above forty. [*Approaching.*] Yet nearer, I don't think so much. [*Approaching.*] By coming close to some women, they look younger still; but when we come very close indeed—

[*Attempting to kiss her.*

Miss Hardcastle. Pray, sir, keep your distance. One would think you wanted to know one's age as they do horses, by mark of mouth.

Marlow. I protest, child, you use me extremely ill. If you keep me at this distance, how is it possible you and I can be ever acquainted?

Miss Hardcastle. And who wants to be acquainted with you? I want no such acquaintance, not I. I'm sure you did not treat

Miss Hardcastle that was here awhile ago in this obstropalous manner. I'll warrant me, before her you look'd dash'd, and kept bowing to the ground, and talk'd, for all the world, as if you was before a justice of peace.

Marlow [*Aside*]. Egad! she has hit it, sure enough. [*To her.*] In awe of her, child? Ha! ha! ha! A mere awkward, squinting thing! No, no! I find you don't know me. I laugh'd, and rallied her a little; but I was unwilling to be too severe. No, I could not be too severe, curse me!

Miss Hardcastle. O! then, sir, you are a favourite, I find, among the ladies?

Marlow. Yes, my dear, a great favourite. And yet, hang me, I don't see what they find in me to follow. At the Ladies' Club in town I'm called their agreeable Rattle. Rattle, child, is not my real name, but one I'm known by. My name is Solomons. Mr. Solomons, my dear, at your service. [*Offering to salute her.*

Miss Hardcastle. Hold, sir; you were introducing me to your club, not to yourself. And you're so great a favourite there you say?

Marlow. Yes, my dear. There's Mrs. Mantrap, Lady Betty Blackleg, the Countess of Sligo, Mrs. Longhorns, old Miss Biddy Buckskin, and your humble servant, keep up the spirit of the place.

Miss Hardcastle. Then it's a very merry place, I suppose.

71

Marlow. Yes, as merry as cards, suppers, wine, and old women can make us.

Miss Hardcastle. And their agreeable Rattle, ha! ha! ha!

Marlow [*Aside*]. Egad! I don't quite like this chit. She looks knowing, methinks. You laugh, child!

Miss Hardcastle. I can't but laugh to think what time they all have for minding their work or their family.

Marlow [*Aside*]. All's well, she don't laugh at me. [*To her.*] Do *you* ever work, child?

Miss Hardcastle. Ay, sure. There's not a screen or a quilt in the whole house but what can bear witness to that.

Marlow. Odso! Then you must show me your embroidery. I

embroider and draw patterns myself a little. If you want a judge of your work you must apply to me. *[Seizing her hand.*

Enter HARDCASTLE, *who stands in surprise.*

Miss Hardcastle. Ay, but the colours don't look well by candle light. You shall see all in the morning. *[Struggling.*

Marlow. And why not now, my angel? Such beauty fires beyond the power of resistance.—Pshaw! the father here! My old luck: I never nick'd seven that I did not throw ames-ace* three times following. *[Exit* MARLOW.

*Dice terms; ames-ace is a pair of ones.

Hardcastle. So, madam! So I find *this* is your *modest* lover. This is your humble admirer that kept his eyes fixed on the ground, and only ador'd at humble distance. Kate, Kate, art thou not asham'd to deceive your father so?

Miss Hardcastle. Never trust me, dear papa, but he's still the modest man I first took him for; you'll be convinced of it as well as I.

Hardcastle. By the hand of my body, I believe his impudence is infectious! Didn't I see him seize your hand? Didn't I see him haul you about like a milk maid? And now you talk of his respect and his modesty, forsooth!

Miss Hardcastle. But if I shortly convince you of his modesty, that he has only the faults that will pass off with time, and the virtues that will improve with age, I hope you'll forgive him.

73

Hardcastle. The girl would actually make one run mad! I tell you I'll not be convinced. I am convinced. He has scarcely been three hours in the house, and he has already encroached on all my prerogatives. You may like his impudence, and call it modesty. But my son-in-law, madam, must have very different qualifications.

Miss Hardcastle. Sir, I ask but this night to convince you.

Hardcastle. You shall not have half the time, for I have thoughts of turning him out this very hour.

Miss Hardcastle. Give me that hour then, and I hope to satisfy you.

Hardcastle. Well, an hour let it be then. But I'll have no trifling with our father. All fair and open, do you mind me?

Miss Hardcastle. I hope, sir, you have ever found that I considered your commands as my pride; for your kindness is such that my duty as yet has been inclination.   [*Exeunt.*

✥ ACT FOUR ✥

Scene—*The House*

Enter Hastings *and* Miss Neville.

Hastings. You surprise me! Sir Charles Marlow expected here this night? Where have you had your information?

Miss Neville. You may depend upon it. I just saw his letter to Mr. Hardcastle, in which he tells him he intends setting out a few hours after his son.

Hastings. Then, my Constance, all must be completed before he arrives. He knows me; and should he find me here, would discover my name, and perhaps my designs, to the rest of the family.

Miss Neville. The jewels, I hope, are safe.

Hastings. Yes, yes. I have sent them to Marlow, who keeps the keys of our baggage. In the meantime, I'll go to prepare matters for our elopement. I have had the Squire's promise of a fresh pair of horses; and, if I should not see him again, will write him further directions.   [*Exit.*

Miss Neville. Well, success attend you! In the meantime, I'll

go amuse my aunt with the old pretence of a violent passion for my cousin.
[*Exit.*

Enter MARLOW, *followed by a* SERVANT.

Marlow. I wonder what Hastings could mean by sending me so valuable a thing as a casket to keep for him, when he knows the only place I have is the seat of a post-coach at an inn-door. Have you deposited the casket with the landlady, as I ordered you? Have you put it into her own hands?

Servant. Yes, your honour.

Marlow. She said she'd keep it safe, did she?

Servant. Yes, she said she'd keep it safe enough; she ask'd me how I came by it, and she said she had a great mind to make me give an account of myself.
[*Exit* SERVANT.

Marlow. Ha! Ha! Ha! They're safe, however. What an unaccountable set of beings have we got amongst! This little barmaid, though, runs in my head most strangely, and drives out the absurdities of all the rest of the family. She's mine, she must be mine, or I'm greatly mistaken!

Enter HASTINGS.

Hastings. Bless me! I quite forgot to tell her that I intended to prepare at the bottom of the garden. Marlow here, and in spirits too!

76

Marlow. Give me joy, George! Crown me, shadow me with laurels! Well, George, after all, we modest fellows don't want for success among the women.

Hastings. Some women, you mean. But what success has your honour's modesty been crowned with now that it grows so insolent upon us?

Marlow. Didn't you see the tempting, brisk, lovely little thing that runs about the house with a bunch of keys to its girdle?

Hastings. Well! and what then?

Marlow. She's mine, you rogue, you. Such fire, such motion, such eyes, such lips—but egad! she would not let me kiss them though.

Hastings. But are you sure, so very sure of her?

Marlow. Why, man, she talk'd of showing me her work above-stairs, and I am to improve the pattern.

Hastings. But how can *you*, Charles, go about to rob a woman of her honour?

Marlow. Pshaw! pshaw! we all know the honour of the barmaid of an inn. I don't intend to *rob* her, take my word for it; there's nothing in this house I shan't honestly *pay* for!

Hastings. I believe the girl has virtue.

Marlow. And if she has, I should be the last man in the world that would attempt to corrupt it.

77

Hastings. You have taken care, I hope, of the casket I sent you to lock up? It's in safety?

Marlow. Yes, yes. It's safe enough. I have taken care of it. But how could you think the seat of a post-coach at an inn-door a place of safety? Ah! numbskull! I have taken better precautions for you than you did for yourself.—I have—

Hastings. What!

Marlow. I have sent it to the landlady to keep for you.

Hastings. To the landlady!

Marlow. The landlady.

Hastings. You did!

Marlow. I did. She's to be answerable for its forth-coming, you know.

Hastings. Yes, she'll bring it forth with a witness.

Marlow. Wasn't I right? I believe you'll allow that I acted prudently upon this occasion?

Hastings [*Aside*]. He must not see my uneasiness.

Marlow. You seem a little disconcerted, though, methinks. Sure nothing has happened?

Hastings. No, nothing. Never was in better spirits in all my life. And so you left it with the landlady, who, no doubt, very readily undertook the charge?

Marlow. Rather too readily. For she not only kept the casket,

78

but, thro' her great precaution, was going to keep the messenger too. Ha! ha! ha!

Hastings. He! he! he! They're safe, however.

Marlow. As a guinea in a miser's purse.

Hastings. [*Aside*]. So now all hopes of fortune are at an end, and we must set off without it. [*To him.*] Well, Charles, I'll leave you to your meditations on the pretty bar-maid, and, he! he! he! may you be as successful for yourself as you have been for me.   [*Exit.*

Marlow. Thank ye, George! I ask no more. Ha! ha! ha!

Enter HARDCASTLE.

Hardcastle. I no longer know my own house. It's turned all topsey-turvey. His servants have got drunk already. I'll bear it no longer—and yet, from my respect for his father, I'll be calm. [*To him.*] Mr. Marlow, your servant. I'm your very humble servant.   [*Bowing low.*

Marlow [*Aside*]. Sir, your humble servant. What's to be the wonder now?

Hardcastle. I believe, sir, you must be sensible, sir, that no man alive ought to be more welcome than your father's son, sir. I hope you think so?

Marlow. I do, from my soul, sir. I don't want much entreaty.

79

I generally make my father's son welcome wherever he goes.

Hardcastle. I believe you do, from my soul, sir. But tho' I say nothing to your own conduct, that of your servants is insufferable. Their manner of drinking is setting a very bad example in this house, I assure you.

Marlow. I protest, my very good sir, that's no fault of mine. If they don't drink as they ought, *they* are to blame. I ordered them not to spare the cellar; I did, I assure you. [*To the side scene.*] Here let one of my servants come up. [*To him.*] My positive directions were, that as I did not drink myself, they should make up for my deficiencies below.

Hardcastle. Then they had your orders for what they do! I'm satisfied!

Marlow. They had, I assure you. You shall hear from one of themselves.

Enter SERVANT, *drunk.*

Marlow. You, Jeremy! Come forward, sirrah! What were my orders? Were you not told to drink freely, and call for what you thought fit, for the good of the house?

Hardcastle [*Aside*]. I begin to lose my patience.

Jeremy. Please your honour, liberty and Fleet-street for ever! Tho' I'm but a servant, I'm as good as another man. I'll drink for no man before supper, sir, dammy! Good liquor will sit upon

80

a good supper, but a good supper will not sit upon—hiccup—
upon my conscience, sir.　　　　　　　　　[*Exit* Jeremy.

Marlow. You see, my old friend, the fellow is as drunk as he
can possibly be. I don't know what you'd have more, unless
you'd have the poor devil soused in a beer-barrel.

Hardcastle. Zounds! He'll drive me distracted if I contain myself any longer. Mr. Marlow. Sir; I have submitted to your insolence for more than four hours, and I see no likelihood of its
coming to an end. I'm now resolved to be master here, sir, and
I desire that you and your drunken pack may leave my house
directly.

Marlow. Leave your house!—Sure, you jest, my good friend!
What, when I'm doing what I can to please you!

Hardcastle. I tell you, sir, you don't please me; so I desire you'll leave my house.

Marlow. Sure, you cannot be serious! At this time o' night, and such a night! You only mean to banter me?

Hardcastle. I tell you, sir, I'm serious; and, now that my passions are roused, I say this house is mine, sir; this house is mine, and I command you to leave it directly.

Marlow. Ha! ha! ha! A puddle in a storm. I shan't stir a step, I assure you. [*In a serious tone.*] This your house, fellow! It's my house. This is my house. Mine, while I choose to stay. What right have you to bid me leave this house, sir? I never met with such impudence, curse me, never in my whole life before!

Hardcastle. Nor I, confound me if ever I did! To come to my house, to call for what he likes, to turn me out of my own chair, to insult the family, to order his servants to get drunk, and then to tell me—*This house is mine, sir.* But all that's impudent, it makes me laugh. Ha! ha! ha! Pray, sir, [*bantering*] as you take the house, what think you of taking the rest of the furniture? There's a pair of silver candlesticks, and there's a fire-screen, and here's a pair of brazen nosed bellows, perhaps you may take a fancy to them?

Marlow. Bring me your bill, sir, bring me your bill, and let's make no more words about it.

Hardcastle. There are a set of prints too. What think you of the *Rake's Progress* for your own apartment?

Marlow. Bring me your bill, I say; and I'll leave you and your infernal house directly.

Hardcastle. Then there's a mahogany table, that you may see your face in.

Marlow. My bill, I say.

Hardcastle. I had forgot the great chair, for your own particular slumbers, after a hearty meal.

Marlow. Zounds! Bring me my bill, I say, and let's hear no more on't.

Hardcastle. Young man, young man, from your father's letter to me, I was taught to expect a well-bred, modest man as a visitor here, but now I find him no better than a coxcomb and a bully; but he will be down here presently, and shall hear more of it. ⸤*Exit.*

Marlow. How's this! Sure, I have not mistaken the house? Every thing looks like an inn. The servants cry "Coming." The attendance is awkward; the bar-maid, too, to attend us. But she's here, and will further inform me. Whither so fast, child? A word with you.

Enter Miss Hardcastle.

Miss Hardcastle ⸤*Aside*⸥. Let it be short, then. I'm in a hurry.—I believe he begins to find out his mistake, but it's too soon quite to undeceive him.

Marlow. Pray, child, answer me one question. What are you, and what may your business in this house be?

Miss Hardcastle. A relation of the family, sir.

Marlow. What! A poor relation?

Miss Hardcastle. Yes, sir. A poor relation appointed to keep the keys, and to see that the guests want nothing in my power to give them.

Marlow. That is, you act as the bar-maid of this inn.

Miss Hardcastle. Inn! O law!—What brought that in your head? One of the best families in the county keep an inn! Ha, ha, ha, old Mr. Hardcastle's house an inn!

Marlow. Mr. Hardcastle's house! Is this house Mr. Hardcastle's house, child?

Miss Hardcastle. Ay, sure. Whose else should it be?

Marlow. So then all's out, and I have been damnably imposed on. O, confound my stupid head, I shall be laugh'd at over the whole town. I shall be stuck up in caricatura in all the print-shops. The Dullissimo Maccaroni. To mistake this house of all others for an inn, and my father's old friend for an inn-keeper! What a swaggering puppy must he take me for! What a silly puppy do I find myself! There again, may I be hang'd, my dear, but I mistook you for the bar-maid!

84

Miss Hardcastle. Dear me! dear me! I'm sure there's nothing in my *behaviour* to put me upon a level with one of that stamp.

Marlow. Nothing, my dear, nothing. But I was in for a list of blunders, and could not help making you a subscriber. My stupidity saw every thing the wrong way. I mistook your assiduity for assurance, and your simplicity for allurement. But it's over—this house I no more show my *face* in!

Miss Hardcastle. I hope, sir, I have done nothing to disoblige you. I'm sure I should be sorry to affront any gentleman who has been so polite, and said so many civil things to me. I'm sure I should be sorry [*Pretending to cry*] if he left the family upon my account. I'm sure I should be sorry people said any thing amiss, since I have no fortune but my character.

Marlow [*Aside*]. By heaven, she weeps! This is the first mark of tenderness I ever had from a modest woman, and it touches me. [*To her.*] Excuse me, my lovely girl, you are the only part of the family I leave with reluctance. But to be plain with you, the difference of our birth, fortune and education, make an honourable connexion impossible; and I can never harbour a thought of seducing simplicity that trusted in my honour, or bringing ruin upon one whose only fault was being too lovely.

Miss Hardcastle [*Aside*]. Generous man! I now begin to admire him. [*To him.*] But I'm sure my family is as good as Miss Hardcastle's, and though I'm poor, that's no great misfortune

85

to a contented mind, and, until this moment, I never thought that it was bad to want fortune.

Marlow. And why now, my pretty simplicity?

Miss Hardcastle. Because it puts me at a distance from one that if I had a thousand pound I would give it all to.

Marlow [*Aside*]. This simplicity bewitches me, so that if I stay I'm undone. I must make one bold effort, and leave her. [*To her.*] Your partiality in my favour, my dear, touches me most sensibly, and were I to live for myself alone, I could easily fix my choice. But I owe too much to the opinion of the world, too much to the authority of a father, so that—I can scarcely speak of it—it affects me! Farewell!   [*Exit.*

Miss Hardcastle. I never knew half his merit till now. He shall not go, if I have power or art to detain him. I'll still preserve the character in which I stoop'd to conquer, but will undeceive my papa, who, perhaps, may laugh him out of his resolution.   [*Exit.*

Enter TONY, MISS NEVILLE.

Tony. Ay, you may steal for yourselves the next time. I have done my duty. She has got the jewels again, that's a sure thing; but she believes it was all a mistake of the servants.

Miss Neville. But, my dear cousin, sure you won't forsake us in this distress. If she in the least suspects that I am going off,

86

I shall certainly be locked up, or sent to my Aunt Pedigree's, which is ten times worse.

Tony. To be sure, aunts of all kinds are damn'd bad things. But what can I do? I have got you a pair of horses that will fly like Whistlejacket, and I'm sure you can't say but I have courted you nicely before her face. Here she comes; we must court a bit or two more, for fear she should suspect us.

[*They retire, and seem to fondle.*

Enter MRS. HARDCASTLE.

Mrs. Hardcastle. Well, I was greatly fluttered, to be sure. But my son tells me it was all a mistake of the servants. I shan't be easy, however, till they are fairly married, and then let her keep her own fortune. But what do I see! Fondling together, as I'm alive! I never saw Tony so sprightly before. Ah, have I caught you, my pretty doves? What, billing, exchanging stolen glances, and broken murmurs! Ah!

Tony. As for murmurs, mother, we grumble a little now and then, to be sure. But there's no love lost between us.

Mrs. Hardcastle. A mere sprinkling, Tony, upon the flame, only to make it burn brighter.

Miss Neville. Cousin Tony promises to give us more of his company at home. Indeed, he shan't leave us any more. It won't leave us, Cousin Tony, will it?

Tony. O, it's a pretty creature! No, I'd sooner leave my horse in a pound than leave you when you smile upon one so. Your laugh makes you so becoming.

Miss Neville. Agreeable cousin! Who can help admiring that natural humour, that pleasant, broad, red, thoughtless, [*Patting his cheek*]—ah, it's a bold face!

Mrs. Hardcastle. Pretty innocence!

Tony. I'm sure I always lov'd Cousin Con's hazel eyes, and her pretty long fingers, that she twists this way and that over the haspicholls, like a parcel of bobbins.

Mrs. Hardcastle. Ah, he would charm the bird from the tree. I was never so happy before. My boy takes after his father, Mr.

Lumpkin, exactly. The jewels, my dear Con, shall be yours in-continently. You shall have them. Isn't he a sweet boy, my dear? You shall be married to-morrow, and we'll put off the rest of his education, like Dr. Drowsy's sermons, to a fitter oppor-tunity.

Enter DIGGORY.

Diggory. Where's the 'Squire? I have got a letter for your worship.

Tony. Give it to my mamma. She reads all my letters first.

Diggory. I had orders to deliver it into your own hands.

Tony. Who does it come from?

Diggory. Your worship mun ask that o' the letter itself.

⎡*Exit* DIGGORY.

Tony. I could wish to know, tho'.

⎡*Turning the letter, and gazing on it.*

Miss Neville ⎡*Aside*⎤. Undone, undone! A letter to him from Hastings. I know the hand. If my aunt sees it, we are ruined for ever. I'll keep her employ'd a little if I can. ⎡*To* MRS. HARD-CASTLE.⎤ But I have not told you, madam, of my cousin's smart answer just now to Mr. Marlow. We so laugh'd—You must know, madam—this way a little, for he must not hear us.

⎡*They confer.*

Tony ⎡*Still gazing*⎤. A damn'd cramp piece of penmanship as ever I saw in my life. I can read your print-hand very well.

But here there are such handles, and shanks, and dashes that one can scarce tell the head from the tail. *To Anthony Lumpkin, Esquire.* It's very odd, I can read the outside of my letters, where my own name is, well enough. But when I come to open it, it's all—buzz. That's hard, very hard; for the inside of the letter is always the cream of the correspondence.

Mrs. Hardcastle. Ha! ha! ha! Very well, very well. And so my son was too hard for the philosopher.

Miss Neville. Yes, madam; but you must hear the rest, madam. A little more this way, or he may hear us. You'll hear how he puzzled him again.

Mrs. Hardcastle. He seems strangely puzzled now himself, methinks.

Tony [*Still gazing*]. A damn'd up and down hand, as if it was disguised in liquor. [*Reading.*] *Dear Sir.* Ay that's that. Then there's an *M*, and a *T*, and an *S*, but whether the next be an izzard or an *R*, confound me, I cannot tell!

Mrs. Hardcastle. What's that, my dear? Can I give you any assistance?

Miss Neville. Pray, aunt, let me read it. No body reads a cramp hand better than I. [*Twitching the letter from her.*] Do you know who it is from?

Tony. Can't tell, except from Dick Ginger the feeder.

Miss Neville. Ay, so it is. [*Pretending to read.*]

"DEAR 'SQUIRE,

"Hoping that you're in health, as I am at this present. The gentlemen of the Shake-bag club has cut the gentlemen of Goose-green quite out of feather. The odds—um—odd battle—um—long fighting"—um. Here, here, it's all about cocks, and fighting; it's of no consequence; here, put it up, put it up.

[*Thrusting the crumpled letter upon him.*

Tony. But, I tell you, miss, it's of all the consequence in the world! I would not lose the rest of it for a guinea! Here, mother, do you make it out. Of no consequence!

[*Giving* MRS. HARDCASTLE *the letter.*

Mrs. Hardcastle. How's this! [*Reads.*] "Dear 'Squire, I'm now waiting for Miss Neville, with a post-chaise and pair, at the bottom of the garden, but I find my horses yet unable to perform the journey. I expect you'll assist us with a pair of fresh horses, as you promised. Dispatch is necessary, as the *hag*, (ay, the hag) your mother, will otherwise suspect us. Yours, Hastings." Grant me patience. I shall run distracted! My rage choaks me!

Miss Neville. I hope, madam, you'll suspend your resentment for a few moments, and not impute to me any impertinence or sinister design that belongs to another.

Mrs. Hardcastle [*Curtseying very low*]. Fine spoken, madam; you are most miraculously polite and engaging, and quite the

91

very pink of courtesy and circumspection, madam. [*Changing her tone.*] And you, you great ill-fashioned oaf, with scarce sense enough to keep your mouth shut. Were you, too, join'd against me? But I'll defeat all your plots in a moment. As for you, madam, since you have got a pair of fresh horses ready, it would be cruel to disappoint them. So, if you please, instead of running away with your spark, prepare, this very moment, to run off with *me*. Your old Aunt Pedigree will keep you secure, I'll warrant me. You too, sir, may mount your horse, and guard us upon the way. Here, Thomas, Roger, Diggory! I'll show you that I wish you better than you do yourselves.   [*Exit.*

Miss Neville. So now I'm completely ruined.

Tony. Ay, that's a sure thing.

Miss Neville. What better could be expected from being connected with such a stupid fool,—and after all the nods and signs I made him!

Tony. By the laws, miss, it was your own cleverness, and not my stupidity, that did your business. You were so nice and so busy with your Shake-bags and Goose-greens that I thought you could never be making believe.

Enter HASTINGS.

Hastings. So, sir, I find by my servant that you have shown my letter and betray'd us. Was this well done, young gentleman?

Tony. Here's another. Ask miss there who betray'd you. Ecod, it was her doing; not mine.

Enter MARLOW.

Marlow. So I have been finely used here among you. Rendered contemptible, driven into ill manners, insulted, laugh'd at.

Tony. Here's another. We shall have old Bedlam broke loose presently.

Miss Neville. And there, sir, is the gentleman to whom we all owe every obligation.

Marlow. What can I say to him, a mere boy, an idiot, whose ignorance and age are a protection.

Hastings. A poor contemptible booby that would but disgrace correction.

Miss Neville. Yet with cunning and malice enough to make himself merry with all our embarrassments.

Hastings. An insensible cub.

Marlow. Replete with tricks and mischief.

Tony. Baw! damme, but I'll fight you both one after the other,—with baskets!

Marlow. As for him, he's below resentment. But your conduct, Mr. Hastings, requires an explanation. You knew of my mistakes, yet would not undeceive me.

Hastings. Tortured as I am with my own disappointments, is this a time for explanations? It is not friendly, Mr. Marlow.

Marlow. But, sir—

Miss Neville. Mr. Marlow, we never kept on your mistake, till it was too late to undeceive you. Be pacified.

Enter SERVANT.

Servant. My mistress desires you'll get ready immediately, madam. The horses are putting to. Your hat and things are in the next room. We are to go thirty miles before morning.

[*Exit* SERVANT.

Miss Neville. Well, well; I'll come presently.

Marlow [*To* HASTINGS]. Was it well done, sir, to assist in rendering me ridiculous? To hang me out for the scorn of all my acquaintance? Depend upon it, sir, I shall expect an explanation.

Hastings. Was it well done, sir, if you're upon that subject, to deliver what I entrusted to yourself to the care of another, sir?

Miss Neville. Mr. Hastings. Mr. Marlow. Why will you increase my distress by this groundless dispute? I implore you— I entreat you—

Enter SERVANT.

Servant. Your cloak, madam. My mistress is impatient.

Miss Neville. I come. [*Exit* SERVANT.] Pray be pacified. If I leave you thus, I shall die with apprehension!

94

Enter SERVANT.

Servant. Your fan, muff, and gloves, madam. The horses are waiting.

Miss Neville. O, Mr. Marlow! if you knew what a scene of constraint and ill-nature lies before me, I'm sure it would convert your resentment into pity.

Marlow. I'm so distracted with a variety of passions that I don't know what I do. Forgive me, madam. George, forgive me. You know my hasty temper, and should not exasperate it.

Hastings. The torture of my situation is my only excuse.

Miss Neville. Well, my dear Hastings, if you have that esteem for me that I think, that I am sure you have, your con-

95

stancy for three years will but increase the happiness of our future connexion. If—

Mrs. Hardcastle [*Within*]. Miss Neville Constance, why, Constance, I say.

Miss Neville. I'm coming. Well, constancy. Remember, constancy is the word.   [*Exit, followed by the* SERVANT.

Hastings. My heart! How can I support this! To be so near happiness, and such happiness!

Marlow [*To* TONY]. You see now, young gentleman, the effects of your folly. What might be amusement to you is here disappointment, and even distress.

Tony [*From a reverie*]. Ecod, I have hit it. It's here. Your hands. Your and yours, my poor Sulky. My boots there, ho! Meet me two hours hence at the bottom of the garden; and if you don't find Tony Lumpkin a more good-natur'd fellow than you thought for, I'll give you leave to take my best horse, and Bet Bouncer into the bargain! Come along. My boots, ho!

[*Exeunt.*

❧ ACT FIVE ❧

SCENE I—*Continues*

Enter HASTINGS *and* SERVANT.

HASTINGS. You saw the old lady and Miss Neville drive off, you say?

Servant. Yes, your honour. They went off in a post coach, and the young 'Squire went on horseback. They're thirty miles off by this time.

Hastings. Then all my hopes are over.

Servant. Yes, sir. Old Sir Charles is arrived. He and the old gentleman of the house have been laughing at Mr. Marlow's mistake this half hour. They are coming this way.

Hastings. Then I must not be seen. So now to my fruitless appointment at the bottom of the garden. This is about the time.

[*Exit.*

Enter SIR CHARLES *and* HARDCASTLE.

Hardcastle. Ha! ha! ha! The peremptory tone in which he sent forth his sublime commands.

97

Sir Charles. And the reserve with which I suppose he treated all your advances.

Hardcastle. And yet he might have seen something in me above a common inn-keeper too.

Sir Charles. Yes, Dick, but he mistook you for an uncommon inn-keeper, ha! ha! ha!

Hardcastle. Well, I'm in too good spirits to think of any thing but joy. Yes, my dear friend, this union of our families will make our personal friendships hereditary: and tho' my daughter's fortune is but small—

Sir Charles. Why, Dick, will you talk of fortune to *me?* My son is possessed of more than a competence already, and can want nothing but a good and virtuous girl to share his happiness and increase it. If they like each other, as you say they do—

Hardcastle. If, man! I tell you they *do* like each other. My daughter as good as told me so.

Sir Charles. But girls are apt to flatter themselves, you know.

Hardcastle. I saw him grasp her hand in the warmest manner myself; and here he comes to put you out of your *ifs,* I warrant him.

Enter MARLOW.

Marlow. I come, sir, once more, to ask pardon for my strange conduct. I can scarce reflect on my insolence without confusion.

Hardcastle. Tut, boy, a trifle. You take it too gravely. An

98

hour or two's laughing with my daughter will set all to rights again. She'll never like you the worse for it.

Marlow. Sir, I shall be always proud of her approbation.

Hardcastle. Approbation is but a cold word, Mr. Marlow; if I am not deceived, you have something more than approbation thereabouts. You take me.

Marlow. Really, sir, I have not that happiness.

Hardcastle. Come, boy, I'm an old fellow, and know what's what as well as you that are younger. I know what has past between you; but mum.

Marlow. Sure, sir, nothing has past between us but the most profound respect on my side, and the most distant reserve on hers. You don't think, sir, that my impudence has been past upon all the rest of the family?

Hardcastle. Impudence! No, I don't say that—Not quite impudence—Though girls like to be play'd with, and rumpled a little, too, sometimes. But she has told no tales, I assure you.

Marlow. I never gave her the slightest cause.

Hardcastle. Well, well, I like modesty in its place well enough. But this is over-acting, young gentleman. You *may* be open. Your father and I will like you the better for it.

Marlow. May I die, sir, if I ever—

Hardcastle. I tell you, she don't dislike you; and as I'm sure you like her—

Marlow. Dear sir—I protest, sir—

Hardcastle. I see no reason why you should not be joined as fast as the parson can tie you.

Marlow. But hear me, sir—

Hardcastle. Your father approves the match, I admire it, every moment's delay will be doing mischief, so—

Marlow. But why won't you hear me? By all that's just and true, I never gave Miss Hardcastle the slightest mark of my attachment, or even the most distant hint to suspect me of affection. We had but one interview, and that was formal, modest, and uninteresting.

Hardcastle [*Aside*]. This fellow's formal, modest impudence is beyond bearing.

Sir Charles. And you never grasp'd her hand, or made any protestations!

Marlow. As Heaven is my witness, I came down in obedience to your commands. I saw the lady without emotion, and parted without reluctance. I hope you'll exact no further proofs of my duty, nor prevent me from leaving a house in which I suffer so many mortifications. [*Exit.*

Sir Charles. I'm astonish'd at the air of sincerity with which he parted.

Hardcastle. And I'm astonish'd at the deliberate intrepidity of his assurance.

Sir Charles. I dare pledge my life and honour upon his truth.

Hardcastle. Here comes my daughter, and I would stake my happiness upon her veracity.

Enter MISS HARDCASTLE.

Hardcastle. Kate, come hither, child. Answer us sincerely, and without reserve; has Mr. Marlow made you any professions of love and affection?

Miss Hardcastle. The question is very abrupt, sir! But since you require unreserved sincerity, I think he has.

Sir Charles. And pray, madam, have you and my son had more than one interview?

Miss Hardcastle. Yes, sir, several.

Hardcastle [*To* SIR CHARLES]. You see.

Sir Charles. But did he profess any attachment?

Miss Hardcastle. A lasting one.

Sir Charles. Did he talk of love?

Miss Hardcastle. Much, sir.

Sir Charles. Amazing. And all this formally?

Miss Hardcastle. Formally.

Hardcastle. Now, my friend, I hope you are satisfied.

Sir Charles. And how did he behave, madam?

Miss Hardcastle. As most profest admirers do. Said some civil things of my face, talked much of his want of merit, and the

101

greatness of mine; mentioned his heart, gave a short tragedy speech, and ended with pretended rapture.

Sir Charles. Now I'm perfectly convinced, indeed. I know his conversation among women to be modest and submissive. This forward, canting, ranting manner by no means describes him, and I am confident he never sat for the picture.

Miss Hardcastle. Then what, sir, if I should convince you to your face of my sincerity? If you and my papa, in about half an hour, will place yourselves behind that screen, you shall hear him declare his passion to me in person.

Sir Charles. Agreed. And if I find him what you describe, all my happiness in him must have an end.   [*Exit.*

Miss Hardcastle. And if you don't find him what I describe— I fear my happiness must never have a beginning.   [*Exeunt.*

SCENE II—*Changes to the back of the garden*

Enter HASTINGS.

HASTINGS. What an idiot am I, to wait here for a fellow who probably takes a delight in mortifying me. He never intended to be punctual and I'll wait no longer. What do I see? It is he, and perhaps with news of my Constance.

Enter TONY, *booted and spattered.*

Hastings. My honest 'Squire! I now find you a man of your word. This looks like friendship.

Tony. Ay, I'm your friend, and the best friend you have in the world, if you knew but all. This riding by night, by the bye, is cursedly tiresome. It has shook me worse than the basket of a stage-coach.

Hastings. But how? Where did you leave your fellow travellers? Are they in safety? Are they housed?

Tony. Five and twenty miles in two hours and a half is no such bad driving. The poor beasts have smoked for it: rabbet me, but I'd rather ride forty miles after a fox than ten with such *varment*.

Hastings. Well, but where have you left the ladies? I die with impatience.

Tony. Left them? Why, where should I leave them but where I found them?

Hastings. This is a riddle.

Tony. Riddle me this, then. What's that goes round the house, and round the house, and never touches the house?

Hastings. I'm still astray.

Tony. Why, that's it, mon. I have led them astray. By jingo, there's not a pond or slough within five miles of the place but they can tell the taste of.

Hastings. Ha, ha, ha, I understand; you took them in a round while they supposed themselves going forward. And so you have at last brought them home again.

Tony. You shall hear. I first took them down Featherbed-lane, where we stuck fast in the mud. I then rattled them crack over the stones of Up-and-down Hill—I then introduc'd them to the gibbet on Heavy-tree Heath, and from that, with a circum-bendibus, I fairly lodged them in the horse-pond at the bottom of the garden.

Hastings. But no accident, I hope.

Tony. No, no. Only mother is confoundedly frightened. She

thinks herself forty miles off. She's sick of the journey, and the cattle can scarce crawl. So, if your own horses be ready, you may whip off with Cousin, and I'll be bound that no soul here can budge a foot to follow you.

Hastings. My dear friend, how can I be grateful?

Tony. Ay, now its "dear friend," "noble 'Squire." Just now, it was all "idiot," "cub," and run me through the guts. Damn *your* way of fighting, I say. After we take a knock in this part of the country, we kiss and be friends. But if you had run me through the guts, then I should be dead, and you might go kiss the hangman.

Hastings. The rebuke is just. But I must hasten to relieve Miss Neville; if you keep the old lady employed, I promise to take care of the young one.

Tony. Never fear me. Here she comes. Vanish. [*Exit* HAST-INGS]. She's got from the pond, and draggled up to the waist like a mermaid.

Enter MRS. HARDCASTLE.

Mrs. Hardcastle. Oh, Tony, I'm killed. Shook. Battered to death. I shall never survive it. That last jolt that laid us against the quickset hedge has done my business.

Tony. Alack, mama, it was all your own fault. You would be for running away by night, without knowing one inch of the way.

Mrs. Hardcastle. I wish we were at home again. I never met so many accidents in so short a journey. Drench'd in the mud, overturn'd in a ditch, stuck fast in a slough, jolted to a jelly, and at last to lose our way! Whereabouts do you think we are, Tony?

Tony. By my guess we should be upon Crackskull Common, about forty miles from home.

Mrs. Hardcastle. O lud! O lud! the most notorious spot in all the country. We only want a robbery to make a complete night on't.

Tony. Don't be afraid, mama, don't be afraid. Two of the five that kept here are hanged, and the other three may not find us. Don't be afraid. Is that a man that's galloping behind us? No; it's only a tree. Don't be afraid.

Mrs. Hardcastle. The fright will certainly kill me.

Tony. Do you see any thing like a black hat moving behind the thicket?

Mrs. Hardcastle. Oh death!

Tony. No, it's only a cow. Don't be afraid, mama, don't be afraid.

Mrs. Hardcastle. As I'm alive, Tony, I see a man coming towards us. Ah! I'm sure on't. If he perceives us, we are undone.

Tony [*Aside*]. Father-in-law, by all that's unlucky, come to take one of his night walks. [*To her.*] Ah, it's a highwayman,

106

with pistols as long as my arm. A damn'd ill-looking fellow.

Mrs. Hardcastle. Good Heaven defend us! He approaches.

Tony. Do you hide yourself in that thicket, and leave me to manage him. If there be any danger, I'll cough and cry hem. When I cough be sure to keep close.

[MRS. HARDCASTLE *hides behind a tree in the back scene.*]

Enter HARDCASTLE.

Hardcastle. I'm mistaken, or I heard voice of people in want of help. Oh, Tony, is that you? I did not expect you so soon back. Are your mother and her charge in safety?

Tony. Very safe, sir, at my Aunt Pedigree's. Hem.

Mrs. Hardcastle [*From behind*]. Ah, death! I find there's danger.

Hardcastle. Forty miles in three hours; sure that's too much, my youngster.

Tony. Stout horses and willing minds make short journeys, as they say. Hem.

Mrs. Hardcastle [*From behind*]. Sure he'll do the dear boy no harm.

Hardcastle. But I heard a voice here; I should be glad to know from whence it came?

Tony. It was I, sir, talking to myself, sir. I was saying that forty miles in four hours was very good going. Hem. As to be sure it was. Hem. I have got a sort of cold by being out in the air. We'll go in, if you please. Hem.

Hardcastle. But if you talk'd to yourself, you did not answer yourself. I am certain I heard two voices, and am resolved [*Raising his voice*] to find the other out.

Mrs. Hardcastle [*From behind*]. Oh, he's coming to find me out! Oh!

Tony. What need you go, sir, if I tell you? Hem. I'll lay down my life for the truth—hem—I'll tell you all, sir.

[*Detaining him.*

Hardcastle. I tell you I will not be detained. I insist on seeing. It's in vain to expect I'll believe you.

Mrs. Hardcastle [*Running forward from behind*]. O lud, he'll

murder my poor boy, my darling. Here, good gentleman, whet your rage upon me. Take my money, my life, but spare that young gentleman, spare my child, if you have any mercy.

Hardcastle. My wife, as I'm a Christian! From whence can she come, or what does she mean?

Mrs. Hardcastle [*Kneeling*]. Take compassion on us, good Mr. Highwayman. Take our money, our watches, all we have, but spare our lives. We will never bring you to justice, indeed we won't, good Mr. Highwayman.

Hardcastle. I believe the woman's out of her senses. What, Dorothy, don't you know *me?*

Mrs. Hardcastle. Mr. Hardcastle, as I'm alive! My fears blinded me. But, who, my dear, could have expected to meet you here, in this frightful place, so far from home. What has brought you to follow us?

Hardcastle. Sure, Dorothy, you have not lost your wits! So far from home, when you are within forty yards of your own door! [*To him.*] This is one of your old tricks, you graceless rogue, you! [*To her.*] Don't you know the gate, and the mulberry-tree; and don't you remember the horsepond, my dear?

Mrs. Hardcastle. Yes, I shall remember the horsepond as long as I live; I have caught my death in it. [*To* Tony.] And is it to you, you graceless varlet, I owe all this? I'll teach you to abuse your mother, I will.

Tony. Ecod, mother, all the parish says you have spoil'd me, and so you may take the fruits on't.

Mrs. Hardcastle. I'll spoil you, I will.

[*Follows him off the stage. Exit.*

Hardcastle. There's morality, however, in his reply. [*Exit.*

Enter HASTINGS *and* MISS NEVILLE.

Hastings. My dear Constance, why will you deliberate thus? If we delay a moment, all is lost for ever. Pluck up a little resolution, and we shall soon be out of the reach of her malignity.

Miss Neville. I find it impossible. My spirits are so sunk with the agitations I have suffered that I am unable to face any new danger. Two or three years' patience will at last crown us with happiness.

Hastings. Such a tedious delay is worse than inconstancy. Let us fly, my charmer. Let us date our happiness from this very moment. Perish fortune. Love and content will increase what we possess beyond a monarch's revenue. Let me prevail.

Miss Neville. No, Mr. Hastings, no. Prudence once more comes to my relief, and I will obey its dictates. In the moment of passion, fortune may be despised, but it ever produces a lasting repentance. I'm resolved to apply to Mr. Hardcastle's compassion and justice for redress.

Hastings. But tho' he had had the will, he has not the power to relieve you.

Miss Neville. But he has influence, and upon that I am resolved to rely.

Hastings. I have no hopes. But since you persist, I must reluctantly obey you.

SCENE III—*Changes to a room at* MR. HARDCASTLE'S

Enter SIR CHARLES *and* MISS HARDCASTLE.

SIR CHARLES. What a situation am I in! If what you say appears, I shall then find a guilty son. If what he says be true, I shall then lose one that, of all others, I most wish'd for a daughter.

Miss Hardcastle. I am proud of your approbation; and, to show I merit it, if you place yourselves as I directed, you shall hear his explicit declaration. But he comes.

Sir Charles. I'll to your father, and keep him to the appointment.   [*Exit* SIR Charles.

Enter MARLOW.

Marlow. Tho' prepar'd for setting out, I come once more to take leave, nor did I, till this moment, know the pain I feel in the separation.

Miss Hardcastle [*In her own natural manner*]. I believe these

111

sufferings cannot be very great, sir, which you can so easily remove. A day or two longer, perhaps, might lessen your uneasiness, by showing the little value of what you now think proper to regret.

Marlow [*Aside*]. This girl every moment improves upon me. [*To her.*] It must not be, madam. I have already trifled too long with my heart. My very pride begins to submit to my passion. The disparity of education and fortune, the anger of a parent, and the contempt of my equals begin to lose their weight, and nothing can restore me to myself but this painful effort of resolution.

Miss Hardcastle. Then go, sir. I'll urge nothing more to detain you. Tho' my family be as good as hers you came down to visit, and my education, I hope, not inferior, what are these advantages without equal affluence? I must remain contented with the slight approbation of imputed merit; I must have only the mockery of your addresses, while all your serious aims are fix'd on fortune.

Enter HARDCASTLE *and* SIR CHARLES *from behind.*

Sir Charles. Here, behind this screen.

Hardcastle. Ay, ay, make no noise. I'll engage my Kate covers him with confusion at last.

Marlow. By heavens, madam, fortune was ever my smallest

consideration. Your beauty at first caught my eye; for who could see that without emotion? But every moment that I converse with you steals in some new grace, heightens the picture, and gives it stronger expression. What at first seem'd rustic plainness, now appears refin'd simplicity. What seem'd forward assurance, now strikes me as the result of courageous innocence and conscious virtue.

Sir Charles. What can it mean? He amazes me!

Hardcastle. I told you how it would be. Hush!

Marlow. I am now determined to stay, madam, and I have too good an opinion of my father's discernment, when he sees you, to doubt his approbation.

Miss Hardcastle. No, Mr. Marlow, I will not, cannot detain you. Do you think I could suffer a connexion in which there is the smallest room for repentance? Do you think I would take the mean advantage of a transient passion to load you with confusion? Do you think I could ever relish that happiness which was acquired by lessening yours?

Marlow. By all that's good, I can have no happiness but what's in your power to grant me. Nor shall I ever feel repentance but in not having seen your merits before. I will stay, even contrary to your wishes; and tho' you should persist to shun me, I will make my respectful assiduities atone for the levity of my past conduct.

Miss Hardcastle. Sir, I must entreat you'll desist. As our acquaintance began, so let it end, in indifference. I might have given an hour or two to levity; but, seriously, Mr. Marlow, do you think I could ever submit to a connexion where *I* must appear mercenary and *you* imprudent? Do you think I could ever catch at the confident addresses of a secure admirer?

Marlow [*Kneeling*]. Does this look like security? Does this look like confidence? No, madam, every moment that shows me your merit only serves to increase my diffidence and confusion. Here let me continue—

Sir Charles. I can hold it no longer. Charles, Charles, how hast thou deceived me! Is this your indifference, your uninteresting conversation!

Hardcastle. Your cold contempt! your formal interview! What have you to say now?

Marlow. That I'm all amazement? What can it mean?

Hardcastle. It means that you can say and unsay things at pleasure. That you can address a lady in private, and deny it in public; that you have one story for us, and another for my daughter!

Marlow. Daughter!—this lady, your daughter!

Hardcastle. Yes, sir, my only daughter. My Kate, whose else should she be?

Marlow. Oh, the devil!

Miss Hardcastle. Yes, sir, that very identical tall, squinting lady you were pleased to take me for. [*Curtseying.*] She that you addressed as the mild, modest, sentimental man of gravity, and the bold, forward, agreeable Rattle of the Ladies Club; ha, ha, ha!

Marlow. Zounds, there's no bearing this; it's worse than death!

Miss Hardcastle. In which of your characters, sir, will you give us leave to address you? As the faltering gentleman, with looks on the ground, that speaks just to be heard, and hates hypocrisy: or the loud, confident creature that keeps it up with

Mrs. Mantrap and old Miss Biddy Buckskin till three in the morning; ha, ha, ha!

Marlow. O, curse on my noisy head. I never attempted to be impudent yet that I was not taken down. I must be gone.

Hardcastle. By the hand of my body, but you shall not. I see it was all a mistake, and I am rejoiced to find it. You shall not, sir, I tell you. I know she'll forgive you. Won't you forgive him, Kate? We'll all forgive you. Take courage, man.

[*They retire, she tormenting him, to the back scene.*

Enter MRS. HARDCASTLE, TONY.

Mrs. Hardcastle. So, so, they're gone off. Let them go. I care not.

Hardcastle. Who gone?

Mrs. Hardcastle. My dutiful niece and her gentleman, Mr. Hastings, from town. He who came down with our modest visitor, here.

Sir Charles. Who, my honest George Hastings? As worthy a fellow as lives, and the girl could not have made a more prudent choice.

Hardcastle. Then, by the hand of my body, I'm proud of the connexion.

Mrs. Hardcastle. Well, if he has taken away the lady, he has not taken her fortune; that remains in this family to console us for her loss.

116

Hardcastle. Sure, Dorothy, you would not be so mercenary?

Mrs. Hardcastle. Ay, that's my affair, not yours.

Hardcastle. But, you know, if your son, when of age, refuses to marry his cousin, her whole fortune is then at her own disposal.

Mrs. Hardcastle. Ay, but he's not of age, and she has not thought proper to wait for his refusal.

Enter HASTINGS *and* MISS NEVILLE.

Mrs. Hardcastle [Aside]. What! returned so soon? I begin not to like it.

Hastings [To HARDCASTLE*].* For my late attempt to fly off with your niece, let my present confusion be my punishment. We are now come back, to appeal from your justice to your humanity. By her father's consent, I first paid her my addresses, and our passions were first founded in duty.

Miss Neville. Since his death, I have been obliged to stoop to dissimulation to avoid oppression. In an hour of levity, I was ready even to give up my fortune to secure my choice. But I'm now recover'd from the delusion, and hope from your tenderness what is denied me from a nearer connexion.

Mrs. Hardcastle. Pshaw, pshaw, this is all but the whining end of a modern novel!

Hardcastle. Be it what it will, I'm glad they're come back to

117

reclaim their due. Come hither, Tony, boy. Do you refuse this lady's hand whom I now offer you?

Tony. What signifies my refusing? You know I can't refuse her till I'm of age, father.

Hardcastle. While I thought concealing your age, boy, was likely to conduce to your improvement, I concurred with your mother's desire to keep it secret. But since I find she turns it to a wrong use, I must now declare, you have been of age these three months.

Tony. Of age! Am I of age, father?

Hardcastle. Above three months.

Tony. Then you'll see the first use I'll make of my liberty. [*Taking* Miss Neville's *hand.*] Witness all men by these presents, that I, Anthony Lumpkin, Esquire, of BLANK place, refuse you, Constantia Neville, spinster, of no place at all, for my true and lawful wife. So Constance Neville may marry whom she pleases, and Tony Lumpkin is his own man again!

Sir Charles. O brave 'Squire!

Hastings. My worthy friend!

Mrs. Hardcastle. My undutiful offspring!

Marlow. Joy, my dear George, I give you joy sincerely. And could I prevail upon my little tyrant here to be less arbitrary, I should be the happiest man alive, if you would return me the favour.

Hastings [*To* Miss Hardcastle]. Come, madam, you are now driven to the very last scene of all your contrivances. I know you like him, I'm sure he loves you, and you must and shall have him.

Hardcastle [*Joining their hands*]. And I say so too. And Mr. Marlow, if she makes as good a wife as she has a daughter, I don't believe you'll ever repent your bargain. So now to supper; to-morrow we shall gather all the poor of the parish about us, and the Mistakes of the Night shall be crowned with a merry morning; so boy, take her; and as you have been mistaken in the mistress, my wish is that you may never be mistaken in the wife.

❧ EPILOGUE ❧

To be spoken in the character of Miss Hardcastle

Well, having stoop'd to conquer with success,
And gain'd a husband without aid from dress,
Still as a bar-maid, I could wish it, too,
As I have conquer'd him to conquer you:
And let me say, for all your resolution,
That pretty bar-maids have done execution.
Our life is all a play, compos'd to please,
"We have our exits and our entrances."
The first act shows the simple country maid,
Harmless and young, of ev'ry thing afraid,
Blushes when hir'd, and with unmeaning action,
I hopes as how to give you satisfaction.
Her second act displays a livelier scene—
Th' unblushing bar-maid of a country inn.
Who whisks about the house, at market caters,
Talks loud, coquets the guests, and scolds the waiters.
Next the scene shifts to town, and there she soars,

120

The chop-house toast of ogling connoisseurs.
On 'Squires and Cits she there displays her arts,
And on the gridiron broils her lovers' hearts—
And as she smiles, her triumphs to complete,
Even Common Councilmen forget to eat.
The fourth act shows her wedded to the 'Squire,
And Madam now begins to hold it higher;
Pretends to taste, at Operas cries *caro*,
And quits her *Nancy Dawson* for *Che Faro*.
Dotes upon dancing, and in all her pride,
Swims round the room, the *Heinel* of Cheapside:
Ogles and leers with artificial skill,
Till having lost in age the power to kill,
She sits all night at cards, and ogles at spadille.
Such, thro' our lives, the eventful history—
The fifth and last act still remains for me.
The Bar-maid now for your protection prays,
Turns female barrister, and pleads for Bays.

This edition of

SHE STOOPS TO CONQUER

has been designed and illustrated by *T. M. CLELAND*

and printed by *CLARKE & WAY* in New York

for the members of *THE LIMITED EDITIONS CLUB*.

There are fifteen hundred copies,

this being number

 1013

and signed by

M Cleland